ITEM
KT-232-387

Animal Rights

Editor: Tracy Biram

Volume 374

independence
educational publishers

First published by Independence Educational Publishers

The Studio, High Green

Great Shelford

Cambridge CB22 5EG

England

© Independence 2020

Copyright

This book is sold subject to the condition that it shall not,
by way of trade or otherwise, be lent, resold, hired out or otherwise
circulated in any form of binding or cover other than that in which it
is published without the publisher's prior consent.

Photocopy licence

The material in this book is protected by copyright. However, the
purchaser is free to make multiple copies of particular articles for instructional
purposes for immediate use within the purchasing institution.
Making copies of the entire book is not permitted.

ISBN-13: 978 1 86168 831 6

Printed in Great Britain

Zenith Print Group

Contents

Introduction

Animal Rights is Volume 374 in the **issues** series. The aim of the series is to offer current, diverse information about important issues in our world, from a UK perspective.

ABOUT ANIMAL RIGHTS

The UK is a nation of animal lovers and increasingly people are considering the welfare and rights of animals around the World. This book explores our relationship with animals and how we use and often, abuse animals. What are animals used for? From companions, to working animals, to food, animals are an important factor in our everyday lives, even if we don't realise it. We will consider how we can make things better for the animals that help make our lives better.

OUR SOURCES

Titles in the **issues** series are designed to function as educational resource books, providing a balanced overview of a specific subject.

The information in our books is comprised of facts, articles and opinions from many different sources, including:

- Newspaper reports and opinion pieces
- Website factsheets
- Magazine and journal articles
- Statistics and surveys
- Government reports
- Literature from special interest groups.

A NOTE ON CRITICAL EVALUATION

Because the information reprinted here is from a number of different sources, readers should bear in mind the origin of the text and whether the source is likely to have a particular bias when presenting information (or when conducting their research). It is hoped that, as you read about the many aspects of the issues explored in this book, you will critically evaluate the information presented.

It is important that you decide whether you are being presented with facts or opinions. Does the writer give a biased or unbiased report? If an opinion is being expressed, do you agree with the writer? Is there potential bias to the 'facts' or statistics behind an article?

ASSIGNMENTS

In the back of this book, you will find a selection of assignments designed to help you engage with the articles you have been reading and to explore your own opinions. Some tasks will take longer than others and there is a mixture of design, writing and research-based activities that you can complete alone or in a group.

FURTHER RESEARCH

At the end of each article we have listed its source and a website that you can visit if you would like to conduct your own research. Please remember to critically evaluate any sources that you consult and consider whether the information you are viewing is accurate and unbiased.

Useful Websites

www.bluecross.org.uk

www.bornfree.org.uk

www.ciwf.org.uk

www.euronews.com

www.fee.org

www.geographical.co.uk

www.globalanimalnetwork.org

www.gov.uk

www.greenecofriend.co.uk

www.hsi.org

www.independent.co.uk

www.inews.co.uk

www.peta.org.uk

www.petplan.co.uk

www.theconversation.com

www.thecourieronline.co.uk

www.worldanimalprotection.org.uk

www.ypte.org.uk

What is animal rights?

People who support animal rights recognise that all animals have an inherent worth – a value completely separate from their usefulness to humans. We believe that every being with a will to live has the right to live free from exploitation and suffering.

Here are a few ways of understanding this vibrant, exciting movement.

It's a philosophy

Animal rights is based on ethical and moral philosophy. It has been discussed by some of the world's most influential thinkers, from historical figures such as Pythagoras and Leonardo da Vinci – who embraced vegetarianism – to Jeremy Bentham, the founder of the utilitarian school of philosophy, who famously identified animals' capacity for suffering as the characteristic that gives them a right to equal consideration.

> **'The question is not "Can they reason?" nor "Can they talk?" but "Can they suffer?"'**
>
> – Jeremy Bentham

All animals have the ability to suffer in the same way and to the same degree that humans do. They feel pain, pleasure, fear, frustration, loneliness and familial love. Whenever we consider doing something that would interfere with their needs, we are morally obligated to take them into account.

In his book *Animal Liberation*, the philosopher Peter Singer states that the basic principle of equality does not require equal treatment – it requires equal consideration. This is an important distinction when talking about animal rights. People often ask if animal rights means that animals should have the right to vote or drive a car. Of course, that would

be silly because those aren't rights that would benefit animals. But animals have the right not to suffer at the hands of humans and to live their lives free from suffering and exploitation because they have an interest in doing so. That is the difference between equal consideration and equal treatment.

It's intuitive

You don't have to be a philosopher to know that hurting animals is wrong. At its core, animal rights is simple. It's about being kind to others – whether they're members of our own species or not. Almost everyone cares about animals in some context, whether it's a beloved family companion, an irresistibly cute kitten or a majestic wild animal seen in a documentary. After all, we each have some built-in capacity for empathy and compassion, as can be seen from the lengths that children often go to in order to help animals. Logically and morally, there's no reason to differentiate in the way we treat the animals we share our homes with and those who are farmed for food. They're all individuals, with the same capacity to feel pain and fear. Animal rights helps us to look past the arbitrary distinctions between different species, to rediscover our innate compassion and to respect all animals equally.

> **'When it comes to pain, love, joy, loneliness and fear, a rat is a pig is a dog is a boy. Each one values his or her life and fights the knife.'**
>
> – PETA founder Ingrid E. Newkirk

It's a way of life

There's nothing abstract about animal rights, and there are no barriers to getting involved. Anyone who cares about animals can start putting these principles into practice every single day with the food they eat, the clothes they wear and the products they buy. These choices are a form of nonviolent protest that makes a real difference both by reducing the profits of corporations that harm or kill animals and by creating a growing market for cruelty-free food, fashion, services and entertainment.

> ### 'Never doubt that a small group of thoughtful, committed citizens can change the world.'
> ### — Margaret Mead

It's a social movement

Like other major social movements, animal rights brings people together from across political, religious and cultural boundaries to fight against injustice. And like those movements, it's also about fairness. Only prejudice allows us to deny others the rights that we expect to have for ourselves. Whether it's based on race, gender, sexual orientation or species, prejudice is morally unacceptable. Alongside the struggles against racism, sexism and homophobia, there's the struggle against speciesism – discrimination against other beings on the basis of their species.

> ### 'Injustice anywhere is a threat to justice everywhere.'
> ### — Dr Martin Luther King Jr

It's the way forward

Society is evolving and becoming fairer all the time. Despite all the people who say change will never happen, most countries in the world have outlawed human slavery and child labour. Recognising the rights of animals is the next stage in our progress towards a fairer world. As biologists and animal behaviourists learn more about animals' intelligence and the complexity of their lives, there's even less excuse for treating them as commodities rather than the sensitive individuals they are. Most of us grew up eating meat, wearing leather and visiting zoos. Yet, just as we've made the mental shift towards a way of life that respects animals, so society as a whole must outgrow the unethical mindset that animals are here for us to use and kill as we please.

> ### 'The greatness of a nation and its moral progress can be judged by the way its animals are treated.'
> ### — Mahatma Gandhi

Animal rights needs you

Animals' voices often go unheard. That's why it's vital that we speak out for them. Please don't settle for a world in which cruelty is the norm – let animal rights into your life, and stand with the millions of people around the world who are doing everything they can to end the exploitation and killing of our fellow Earthlings.

The above information is reprinted with kind permission from PETA.
© 2020 PETA

www.peta.org.uk

Do animals have rights?

Animals are simply unable to discern right actions from wrong ones by applying moral judgments, which is the reason why it is futile to talk about animal rights.

By Filip Steffensen

Since Peter Singer published *Animal Liberation* in 1975, animal rights activists have proposed the idea that animals should be granted the same rights as human beings. Various movements have emerged, and throughout the past decade, endeavours have turned out to be increasingly successful. Referring to scientific studies with animals exhibiting attributes similar to human beings, activists argue that animals are akin to human beings and should thus be protected with the same body of rights. So why is it that animals do not have the same legal status as human beings?

The case for animal rights

The line of reasoning in favour of granting animals equal rights to human beings emphasizes the fact that scientists have found traits in animals we normally associate with human beings. As an example, a group of scientists showed that monkeys demonstrate self-consciousness at the same level as human beings. This has usually served as a justification for human rights, so why don't we—as a minimum—grant equal rights to the most developed animal species? After all, the principle of habeas corpus—derived from the Magna Carta with the intention to prevent unlawful detentions—would protect those species from encroachment and arbitrary violations of rights, thus avoiding painful and degrading treatment.

The fact that some animals exhibit traits similar to human beings certainly provides a strong argument for granting at least some animals rights. But despite convincing scientific evidence, this argument does not provide any philosophical justification of animal rights. An adequate argument for animal rights would require further philosophical inquiry and not only descriptive conclusions. Of course, we can feel reverence and pity for animals being treated badly, but this does not lead to the conclusion that animals should enjoy the same legal status as persons.

Rights and duties

There is a strong reason for maintaining that rights only apply to human beings. While fundamental rights surely are valuable in their nature, they would be worthless without any mechanism to uphold them. That is why we expect other people to respect our rights.

The mechanism that upholds our rights is the fact that other people are constrained by duties in their behaviour towards us. In our everyday lives, we experience numerous situations in which fraudulent or violent persons could profit from violating our rights. Nonetheless, we see—of course, with some exceptions—that individuals cooperate and respect other people's rights. Rights and duties are two sides of the same coin, and one cannot claim to have certain rights without having to comply with corresponding duties.

Rights would merely be well-intended declarations if it were not for our moral duties toward other people.

Thus, rights would merely be well-intended declarations if it were not for our moral duties toward other people. If it is my claim to live freely on my property without intrusion, my neighbour's duty impedes him from violating my right to property and life. Suppose, however, he trespasses on my plot and engages in vandalism on my property. He will then be held accountable through judicial reprisals, for he has violated my property rights and failed his duty to respect my rights. This is completely reasonable, but we will certainly face obstacles if my property was violated by, say, an elephant or a chimpanzee.

If we assume that animals are granted the same legal status as human beings, justice requires that we now drag the culprit to court. For, remember, if our animal has rights, it will logically also have duties. In other words, it is responsible for its own actions. Therefore, it is now subject to the same legal procedures as human beings. This raises embarrassing practical questions, for who will defend the animal in court? And will the animal be able to comprehend what is going on? History provides us with a great variety of absurd trials involving animals.

Europe's history of animal trials

Faced with criminal charges, animals suffered capital punishment for various crimes in early Europe. There are numerous instances of animals that were tortured and hanged for their vicious crimes. Yet some animals were in fact acquitted for their charges during this paradigm of animal trials. For instance, a donkey was acquitted in 1750 after facing charges of bestiality. But although torture and brutal hangings surely have inflicted pain upon supposedly guilty animals, an important question remains: Did those animals understand human law and morality? I stand to question that. It is inconceivable that those animals would comprehend the slightest fraction of the legal code, of moral questions and the procedures in court. And that is exactly the reason why animals do not have rights.

Dragging animals to court surely seems absurd. Nevertheless, granting rights to animals entails exactly this consequence. Because rights and duties are cognate, animals cannot only enjoy being protected by rights. They will also be subject to corresponding duties. But being unable to comprehend those duties and moral foundations, animals cannot have rights. As Roger Scruton writes, the Constitution was written under the assumption that people are familiar with their duties. We know it's wrong to steal, kill, and cheat other people. But animals don't.

Don't worry: we can still treat animals properly

Though I strongly oppose the idea of granting animals the same rights as human beings, this does not conflict with the proposition that animals should be treated properly. I'm sure most readers here find animal cruelty repugnant, but this, however, is not equal to granting animals rights.

As Carl Cohen noted, we can have obligations from special commitments, but that is not the same as saying that animals have particular claims towards us. Animals are simply unable to discern right actions from wrong ones by applying moral judgments, which is the reason why it is futile to talk about animal rights.

I will now leave it up to the reader to imagine a chimpanzee in the dock indicted with, say, charges for vandalism on my property as hypothesized earlier. Wouldn't it be absurd?

23 February 2019

The above information is reprinted with kind permission from The Foundation for Economic Education (FEE).
© 2020 The Foundation for Economic Education (FEE)

www.fee.org

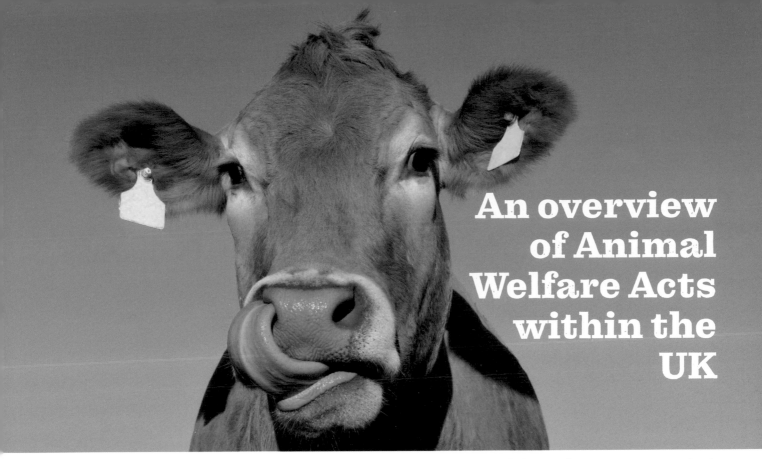

An overview of Animal Welfare Acts within the UK

By choosing to have animals in our care, we have a moral and legal duty of care to ensure their welfare is met. This duty is governed by relevant legislation, dependent on which country we reside in. The UK has three Animal Welfare Acts: one for England and Wales, one for Scotland, and one for Northern Ireland.

Animal welfare issues are devolved within the UK, so the current legislation to protect domestic animals, or captive wild animals under the care of man, falls under the Animal Welfare Act 2006 (England and Wales), the Animal Health and Welfare (Scotland) Act 2006 and the Welfare of Animals (Northern Ireland) Act 2011.

These Acts put the responsibility of the animals' welfare solely onto the owner or care giver, and requires that they must take reasonable steps to meet the animals' basic welfare needs and prevent unnecessary suffering. Failure to do so is an offence, and is prosecutable.

Welfare needs and Codes of Practice

The basic welfare needs of animals under the Animal Welfare Acts are similar to the requirements of the Five Freedoms, and they are as follows:

♦ the need for a suitable environment

♦ the need for a suitable diet

♦ the need to exhibit normal behaviour patterns

♦ the need to be housed with or apart from other animals (as appropriate)

♦ the need to be protected from pain, suffering, injury and disease.

It is the pet owners' responsibility to ensure these needs are being met and to help with this there are associated Codes of Practices which provide care guidelines for cats, dogs, rabbits, equines and non-human primates. These Codes highlight and explain the relevant legal requirements to keep these animals, promote and give examples of good practice, and provide advice on how to best look after your animal. The Codes themselves are not legally binding; however, they can be used to help with prosecutions if welfare needs are not met.

Offences and Prosecutions

A failure to provide adequate care for an animal or causing unnecessary suffering is a breach of the law and can result in a lifetime ban of owning pets, fines up to £20,000 and even prison sentences. However, lack of a licensing or regulatory system means enforcement of these Acts is often difficult.

The above information is reprinted with kind permission from World Animal Protection.
© 2020 World Animal Protection

www.globalanimalnetwork.org

UK loses its A grade in global test of animal welfare leadership

Our Animal Protection Index (API), which ranks countries on their laws protecting animals, exposes the drastic need for global change.

The UK has dropped a grade in a global assessment of countries' records on animal welfare due to Brexit parliamentary delays which have held up planned laws such as animal sentience and export regulation.

The UK previously held an 'A' grade but has now dropped to a 'B' in the second revised edition of the Animal Protection Index (API) which assesses the animal welfare policies and legislation of 50 countries.

The index scores countries from A (being the highest score) to G (being the weakest score) according to their policy and legislation.

'We need stronger laws protecting animals in farming, in entertainment and in homes'.

Shockingly, not one country has obtained an 'A' grade. The United Kingdom is rated highest along with Sweden and Austria all achieving a 'B' score. However, there is room for improvement in these countries too.

Holding countries to account

World Animal Protection is calling on all governments to immediately improve their animal welfare standards, not only for the benefit of animals, but also to reduce the risk to public health.

Sonul Badiani-Hamment, World Animal Protection UK external affairs advisor, said: *'The UK government is failing to keep up with the latest science on animal welfare and has been treading water, making promises of new legislation on animal sentience that have not been met.*

'The UK is a nation of animal lovers and the government must reflect this in their work and continue to improve animal protections if it is to ensure we regain our top rating. We need stronger laws protecting animals in farming, in entertainment and in homes. This is particularly important as the UK leaves the EU, to ensure that hard-won protections are not lost in the rush to agree new trade deals.'

Coronavirus and other concerns

Severe animal welfare concerns from intensive farming, wildlife markets and associated trade are all proven threats of disease outbreak, such as the most recent global epidemic, coronavirus.

The API found that China, USA, Vietnam, Egypt, Azerbaijan and Belarus need to do more to protect animals and people from the threat of zoonotic diseases.

This global threat will continue for as long as there is no effective legislation and preventative measures to control the emerging threat to animal and people's health.

Beyond public health, these systems which put us all at risk are causing immense suffering and cruelty to billions of animals every year.

Does the life of an animal mean nothing at all?

Last year World Animal Protection launched a 60-second film to highlight the many ways that we are failing to protect animals, asking the question: does the life of an animal mean nothing at all?

This is a question we need to ask governments lacking even the most basic animal welfare policies.

10 March 2020

Animal Protection Index

Rankings

A B C D E F G

The above Information is reprinted with kind permission from World Animal Protection.
© 2020 World Animal Protection

www.worldanimalprotection.org.uk

Did you know - owners must make sure their pets are happy by law?

British pet owners have a legal duty to make sure their pets are happy and healthy – but only 35 per cent of them have any idea that this law exists.

I'm already a pet owner, or thinking of getting a pet. What do I need to know?

The Animal Welfare Act 2006 (England and Wales) and Animal Health and Welfare (Scotland) 2006 make a pet owner legally responsible for making sure any domesticated animal under their care has their welfare needs met.

A pet's welfare needs will depend on their species; a cat has very different needs to a tortoise, for example.

What are the five welfare needs?

All domestic animals have the legal right to:

♦ live in a suitable environment

♦ eat a suitable diet

♦ exhibit normal behaviour patterns

♦ be housed with, or apart from, other animals

♦ be protected from pain, suffering, injury and disease

Pet owners must make sure their pet's welfare needs are met, otherwise they could be prosecuted.

You may also hear people referring to the five welfare needs as the 'five freedoms'.

The five welfare needs

Environment

Behaviour

Health

Diet

Companionship

Is the law the same for keeping all pets?

Every domesticated animal who is owned by someone on a temporary or permanent basis has the right to be properly cared for by their owner.

All owners must make sure their pets' welfare needs are met, but these will be different for different pets because different species have different needs.

A horse, for example, may be quite happy living outside all year round if they have access to good shelter. Snakes, however, would not be able to cope with living outdoors in the British climate as they are unable to regulate their own body temperature so need to live in a vivarium with a suitable gradient heat source.

Horses and snakes are different so their specific welfare needs are different, but their owners must make sure they both live in environments that are suitable for them.

What is the punishment for breaking animal welfare law?

Pet owners who fail to ensure their pet's welfare needs are met face prosecution – but importantly, they run the risk of causing suffering to an animal who they have taken into their home and have a responsibility to care for. Failing to meet a pet's welfare needs could cause them to become sick, hurt, upset or stressed.

Owners can be taken to court if they don't look after their pets properly and face a prison sentence of up to six months, and a fine of up to £20,000. They may also have their pet taken away from them, or be banned from having pets in the future.

How can I make sure I am not causing my pet unnecessary suffering?

The vast majority of pet owners love their pets very much and wouldn't dream of doing anything that might cause their pet harm.

Use the five freedoms as a guide. Are you making sure your pet:

1. has a comfy environment to live in that is suitable for their species?
2. gets enough of the right food for their species?
3. has enough space and opportunities to move around as much as they need to?
4. lives with or away from other pets of their own species if they need to?
5. is unlikely to hurt themselves, get sick or suffer?

If the answer to each the above questions is 'yes', you have nothing to worry about. Enjoy having a wonderful bond with your beloved pet!

22 August 2019

The above information is reprinted with kind permission from Blue Cross.
© 2020 Blue Cross

www.bluecross.org.uk

What is animal sentience?

Sentient animals are aware of their feelings and emotions. These could be negative feelings such as pain, frustration and fear. It is logical to suppose that sentient animals also enjoy feelings of comfort, enjoyment, contentment, and perhaps even great delight and joy.

Science shows us some interesting abilities in farm animals:

♦ sheep can recognise up to 50 other sheep's faces and remember them for two years

♦ cows show excitement when they discover how to open a gate leading to a food reward

♦ mother hens teach their chicks which foods are good to eat

♦ lame meat chickens choose to eat food which contains a painkiller.

Scientists believe that sentience is necessary because it helps animals to survive by:

♦ learning more effectively from experience in order to cope with the world

♦ distinguishing and choosing between different objects, animals and situations such as working out who is helpful or who might cause them harm

♦ understanding social relationships and the behaviour of other individuals.

The growing scientific interest in animal sentience is showing what many people have long thought to be the case – that a wide range of animals are thinking, feeling beings. What happens to them matters to them.

'A sentient animal is one for whom feelings matter'

John Webster, Professor Emeritus, University of Bristol

Why animal sentience matters

Animals have evolved to cope as successfully as possible with life in the wild. Thousands of years of domestication of farm animals have changed their basic motivations and behaviour patterns very little.

Industrial-type farming often fails to appreciate animals' needs and their capacity to suffer. This can mean that very large numbers of sentient animals are routinely subjected to pain and deprivation.

Globally each year we farm 70 billion farm animals for meat, milk or eggs. The majority of commercially-farmed animals are confined in cages, narrow stalls or in over-crowded sheds. In such confinement, there is little or no opportunity to carry out the natural behaviours which are so important to them.

It is urgent that farming systems and practices adopt methods which recognise animal sentience and pay full regard to the animals' needs.

The above information is reprinted with kind permission from Compassion in World Farming International.
© 2020 Compassion in World Farming International

www.ciwf.org.uk

Most popular pets in the UK

The UK's most popular pets, revealed.

What's the most popular pet where you live?

Here in the United Kingdom, it's no secret that we are a nation of animal lovers: there is an estimated 51 million pets residing in homes across the UK. Considering that the UK has a population of 66 million, that means there is more than one pet in every other home across the nation – but what is the most sought-after pet in Britain and does pet popularity differ by postcode?

Petplan's *2018 Pet Census*, the largest pet ownership census to date, provides unrivalled insight into the UK's pet-owning households and their furry friends. In celebration of National Pet Month, Petplan takes a look at which pet reigns supreme in the (United) Animal Kingdom and explores if certain regions influence which pet you pick.

Take a look at the infographics to get the lowdown on which pets are most popular near you and read on to discover our *2018 Pet Census* highlights surrounding UK pet popularity.

Earning the title, man's best friend

Using insights from over 60,000 UK pet owners, our *2018 Pet Census* has unearthed that Britain's favourite pet is the dog, winning by a landslide. 67% of our Census respondents were dog owners, though this may come as no surprise due to the long-standing and legendary human-canine bond.

Delving further into pooch popularity, the Labrador Retriever (12%) is top of the charts as the most common canine in UK households, appreciated for its warm, friendly temperament and loyal nature.

Coming in at second place on the pet popularity scale is cats, with 45% of our Census respondents being feline fans. The top kitty of choice is the Moggy (51%), followed by the British Shorthair (24%).

Surprisingly, third place was fish at 9%, closely followed by pets such as rabbits, horses, reptiles, rodents and birds which all averaged between 4% and 2%. However, a significant number of pet owners have more than one type of pet, with 31% owning both a dog and a cat, and 84% of horse owners owning at least one dog.

London's pet preference differs from other UK regions

In almost every area of the country we found that dog ownership far outpaced cat ownership. In some areas, such as Northern Ireland and the North East, this margin was as high as 40% where dog ownership rests at 78% and 75%, respectively. It seems the further north you go, the more popular our canines become.

However, one area that bucked this trend completely was London, with 61% of pet owners living in the capital city owning a cat. Possessing a passion for solo exploring and being independent at heart, felines naturally require less monitored exercise than dogs. Dogs need a lot of exercise, but to get that exercise they also need someone to be with them to keep them safe. Due to Londoners living in a fast-paced, urban environment, it's

Our (United) Animal Kingdom

The practicalities of living in specific regions mean that the UK's most popular pet varies depending on the location in the UK.

Scotland
69% 42% 3% 3% 1%

North East
75% 34% 10% 5% 3%

Northern Ireland
78% 36% 6% 2% 1% 1%

Yorkshire & Humber
67% 45% 9% 4% 3%

North West
70% 42% 10% 4% 2%

East Midlands
69% 42% 9% 5% 3%

West Midlands
72% 41% 5% 3% 2%

East of England
66% 47% 10% 4%

Wales
73% 42% 10% 5% 3%

London
61% 50% 4% 2% 1%

South West
70% 44% 10% 3% 3%

South East
62% 51% 10% 3% 3%

Source: Petplan

London

Cat	Dog	Bird	Rabbit	Horse
61%	50%	4%	2%	1%

Source: Petplan

understandable that cats are preferred for their independent nature.

Dogs are also much larger than cats on average and need bigger home and outdoor spaces to ensure that they live a healthy and happy lifestyle. Whilst cats still thrive within a larger space to roam around, they nonetheless can live happily with less space than dogs and certain breeds are recommended to be kept indoors, including Ragdoll cats.

These factors combined are good indicators of why cat ownership in London is higher than dog ownership. With less room to run around and more expensive properties, cats are much more adapted to urban life, even if they're outdoor cats.

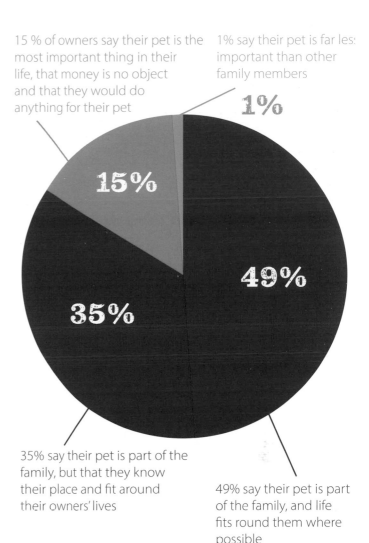

15 % of owners say their pet is the most important thing in their life, that money is no object and that they would do anything for their pet

1% say their pet is far less important than other family members

35% say their pet is part of the family, but that they know their place and fit around their owners' lives

49% say their pet is part of the family, and life fits round them where possible

Source: Petplan

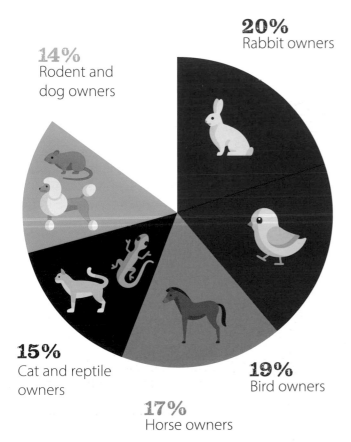

20%
Rabbit owners

14%
Rodent and dog owners

15%
Cat and reptile owners

17%
Horse owners

19%
Bird owners

Source: Petplan

Pets are the family we choose

Providing an unrivalled level of insight into the lives and attitudes of the UK's pet-owning households and their furry friends, Petplan's *Pet Census* revealed the key theme that pets are the family we choose.

No matter what pet people own, between 10 and 20% of owners would always arrange their lives around their pets. Though dogs may spring to mind as requiring the most family adaptation, surprisingly rabbit owners (20%) are the most likely to fit their lives around their pets.

From this we can infer that while dogs and cats may be the most popular, it seems that rabbit owners are the most passionate about their pets being a big part of their family life.

Our Census also uncovered that 49% of UK pet owners have stated that they believe their pet is a family member and 37% of pet owners have stated that they put their pet's needs above their own.

It's easy to see where our animal-loving reputation comes from when the numbers are in front of you.

2018

The above information is reprinted with kind permission from Petplan.
© 2020 Petplan

www.petplan.co.uk

Britain is a nation of pet lovers – and it has the Victorians to thank

An article from *The Conversation.*

THE CONVERSATION

By Jane Hamlett, Professor of Modern British History, Royal Holloway

Britain was the first country in the world to start a welfare charity for animals, as early as 1824. Now, almost 20 million cats and dogs have a loving place in the country's homes, and almost one in two households is accompanied by a furry, scaly or feathered friend.

As a historian of family and home life in 19th- and 20th-century Britain, I've been trying to find out how this came about. With Julie-Marie Strange and our research team, Luke Kelly, Lesley Hoskins and Rebecca Preston, we've been exploring archives from the Victorian era and beyond to figure out how and when pets became so prominent in family life.

Humans have interacted and engaged with animals for thousands of years, but pet-keeping didn't become socially acceptable in Britain until the 18th century. Until then, pets were often seen as an elite extravagance, and small dogs frequently appeared in satirical prints of aristocratic ladies, symbolising frivolity and indulgence.

By the late 18th and early 19th centuries there were fewer of these kinds of images. Instead, paintings and illustrations – a good indicator of what was culturally 'in' – began to portray pets as an accepted part of domestic life.

In part, this was because of the new emphasis Victorians placed on home and domestic life. Responding to the growth of noisy and dirty industrial cities, Victorians began to idealise the home as a sacrosanct space. Pets were a key part of this celebration of domestic life, appearing in numerous paintings and illustrations and often portrayed as part of the family. This was the clear message behind Frederick George Cotman's painting, *One of the Family*, which shows a rural family at the dinner table, accompanied by a pet dog and a horse.

In tandem, a rising Evangelical religious movement placed more emphasis on mothers and fathers in bringing up moral children. In this cultural climate, pet keeping took on a new moral value. From the 1840s, advice books and children's literature encouraged children to keep small animals such as rabbits, guinea pigs and birds. The idea was to cultivate commitment, caring values and practical skills. Boys in particular were expected to learn kindness from these activities.

Victorians kept pets for a variety of reasons. Pedigree dogs conveyed class and status, cats caught mice, and rabbits could be eaten when times were hard. But evidence from interviews, diaries, photographs and the numerous newly created pet cemeteries suggests that, above all, emotional attachment was a crucial part of the relationship between most Victorians and their pets.

Dogs, for example, were held to have virtuous characteristics that echoed the values of the Victorian human world – they were seen as steadfast, loyal and courageous. In the popular painting by Briton Riviere, a little girl, perhaps banished to the naughty step, is accompanied by a faithful dog.

Not all rosy

While the Victorians celebrated pets, there was less consciousness of the harm that might be caused to animals by removing them from their

natural habits. Mice, rabbits, squirrels, hedgehogs and all kinds of British birds regularly featured in advice manuals as animals that could be captured and tamed.

Hedgehogs, for example, were frequently captured and sold at London's Leadenhall Market. Their willingness to eat black beetles made them valuable in London kitchens as they were thought to improve cleanliness. But as how to care for and feed them was not well understood, they tended not to survive for long.

Birds played an important part in working class culture. Though some families kept them in poor conditions, most cared for them fondly, valuing the song, movement, and colour they added to home life. Removing them from the wild was more contentious than other animals – in the 1870s, legislation was passed to limit their capture to certain times of year. However, markets trading in wild birds continued to operate well into the 20th century.

A new century, a new relationship

Taking animals directly from the wild became gradually less acceptable in the 20th century. Changes in living conditions in the early 20th century also altered the way people kept domesticated pets. The building of new suburban houses with larger gardens in the interwar period created a new, more spacious environment for animals. An increasing urban population was encouraged to take in pets that didn't mind living exclusively indoors, such as pedigree cats.

Disposable incomes rose, so there was also more money for people to spend on their companions. After the Second World War, vet services grew, as did companies supplying bespoke food, toys and pampering experiences.

A stronger emphasis developed on building a relationship with pets, rather than simply caring for them. From the 1920s, commentators increasingly wrote of relationships between humans and pets, and of training as an important facet of dog ownership.

By the 1950s, popular animal experts like Barbara Woodhouse were emphasising that owners also had to be trained. Woodhouse argued that 'delinquent canines' - dogs that stole Sunday joints, occupied the favourite chairs of owners or refused to move from their beds – were due to the failings of owners who had not forged meaningful relationships with them.

By the late 1950s and early 1960s, academics had started exploring the significance of pets in family life. Sociologists Harold Bridger and Stephanie White argued in 1964 that the decline of the traditional 'close-knit' family made pets more necessary to bind families together. They predicted that pets would keep becoming more popular long into the future. The booming pet culture in the 21st century appears to fulfil that prophecy.

3 October 2019

The above information is reprinted with kind permission from The Conversation.
© 2010-2020, The Conversation Trust (UK) Limited

www.theconversation.com

Animal Experimentation

Chapter 2

Vivisection

Vivisection is the practice of using animals for scientific and medical purposes.

What are the experiments for?

Some reasons for animal experiments include:

♦ Developing treatments for new diseases

♦ Biological and medical research

♦ Safety testing (including of cosmetics)

♦ Animals bred with an inherited genetic defect for medical research

♦ Developing new methods of diagnosis

Which animals are used in research?

Rats, mice and other rodents (bred for research)

Fish, birds, amphibians and reptiles

Small mammals other than rodents mainly rabbits and ferrets

Sheep, cows, pigs and other large mammals

Dogs and cats (bred for research)

Monkeys such as marmosets and macaques

What do experiments on animals prove?

Many animal experiments are performed to highlight any potentially harmful effects of newly-developed medicines and chemical substances on humans. In some cases, researchers try to mimic conditions affecting humans (e.g. cancer, cystic fibrosis, arthritis, etc.) in the animals they are experimenting on, to see if new medicines will be effective in treating them. The Research Defence Society (a pro-vivisection organisation) claims that inherited diseases such as cystic fibrosis are now being accurately reproduced in specially bred genetically altered laboratory mice.

What follows can be seen as the arguments put forward by people with completely opposing views. The anti-vivisectionists claim that vivisection is outdated, unnecessary, cruel and produces misleading results. Pro-vivisectionists say that animal experiments are vital to the advancement of medicine, that care is taken to limit the suffering inflicted on animals and that vivisection is the only accurate way to test responses of entire living organisms to chemicals, rather than those of an isolated section of body tissue.

The arguments against

One of the most serious arguments against animal testing is that the results obtained from experiments on animals do not accurately show the effects of a tested substance on humans. Professor Pietro Croce, an Italian, was a vivisector for many years, and now campaigns against animal testing. Among the examples he gives of animals giving misleading results when compared with humans are:

- Parsley is a deadly poison for parrots.

- Arsenic, a poison to humans is harmless to sheep. Sheep, goats, horses and mice can also eat hemlock in huge quantities - whereas it is a poison to humans.

- A hedgehog can eat enough opium at one sitting to keep a hardened drug addict high for a fortnight.

- Morphine is an anaesthetic for humans, yet if it is given to cats, it produces a state of frenzied excitement.

- Vitamin C is not needed at all by dogs, rats, hamsters and mice, as their bodies produce Vitamin C of their own accord. If humans, primates or guinea-pigs are deprived of Vitamin C, they will die of scurvy.

- Simply inhaling the fumes of prussic acid is enough to kill humans, yet it can be drunk without harm by toads, sheep and hedgehogs.

- Scopolamine can kill humans with a dose of just 5 milligrams. Dogs and cats find 100 milligrams harmless. This is very worrying when it comes to working out safe dosages, as it is calculated by looking at the relationship between body mass and dosage. If we take the average cat to weigh 4 kilograms and the average human to weigh 70 kilograms, this means the correct dose of scopolamine for a human would be 1800 milligrams - 360 times the actual safe dose.

- Penicillin, the first antibiotic, was tested on mice. Had it been tested on guinea pigs, it would have been considered dangerous, as penicillin affects the floral bacteria in guinea pigs' stomachs, and kills them within a few days.

Professor Croce argues that to obtain the result you want from an animal test, you just have to choose the species to carry out the tests on. In this way, health warnings on cigarette packets were held up for years during the 1960s whilst scientists (paid by tobacco companies) proved time and again that smoking cigarettes does not cause lung cancer in rats and mice, despite the fact that by that time, there was already plenty of documented human evidence to show that cigarettes were dangerous!

The unreliability of animal testing was shown to disastrous effect in the case of fialuridine. This drug passed its animal test phase with no problems, but when it was given to fifteen volunteer humans, it caused acute liver damage, killing five of them and forcing two others to have liver transplants. However, this kind of problem is very rare, and must not be seen as representative of all animal testing.

The Medical Research Modernization Committee (MRMC), an American organisation for doctors who are against animal testing, states that vivisection makes it easy for scientists to quickly come up with 'new' and 'exciting' research. All they have to do is take existing data and change the animal species being experimented on to produce a different result. This allows researchers to publish their findings regularly, and enables them to find funding for future research. Frequently though, these experiments produce no data useful to the advance of human medicine.

The MRMC also suggests that trying to learn about treating diseases such as cancer and AIDS using animal testing is a waste of time and money. They claim that since 1971, when the National Cancer Act was passed in the US, billions of dollars have been spent on possible cancer cures, but have yielded little in the way of new treatments. A major reason for this, MRMC suggests, is that cancers in animals develop and progress in very different ways to cancers in humans. In 1986, two time Nobel prize winner Linus Pauling wrote:

'Everyone should know that most cancer research is largely a fraud, and that the major cancer research organisations are derelict in their duties to the people who support them.'

AIDS research in America has also been unproductive, say the MRMC. Animals infected with HIV have failed to develop symptoms similar to those caused by AIDS in humans. Over a ten year period, more than 100 chimpanzees (our closest living relatives) have been infected with HIV. Only two have become ill. The same report goes on to suggest that AIDS may have been caused by vivisection, with monkey viruses being mutated to form HIV whist producing a polio vaccine from baboon tissue. It is certainly true that 15 laboratory workers in the US have been killed by the Marburg virus and other monkey viruses, and that there have been two outbreaks of Ebola in US monkey colonies.

The above is just a small proportion of the evidence and information to be obtained to back up the allegation that animals are unlike humans and should therefore not be used to predict human reactions to new treatments and medicines.

Arguments for

The Research Defence Society (RDS) is a British organisation set up to defend animal testing. It claims that most of the accusations made against vivisection are inaccurate, and that animal testing produces valuable information about how new drugs react inside a living body. Tests are carried out to identify major undesirable effects such as liver damage, raised blood pressure, nerve damage or damage to the foetus. It says that drugs can be altered by digestion, and become either less effective or more toxic, and that such problems cannot be investigated using cell samples in test tubes. Uncaged, MRMC and Professor Croce all argue that in vitro (test tube) experiments are at least as accurate and often more accurate than animal tests.

Albino rabbits are commonly used in the Draize tests, which check for eye irritation. The rabbits are chosen for these tests not because their eyes are similar to human eyes, but because they are cheap to obtain, are unlikely to bite their handlers and have relatively large eyes which are easy to observe. Rabbits have different eyelid and cornea structure to humans, and are less able to produce tears, making the Draize tests unreliable in predicting human toxicity.

All mammals, says the RDS, have the same organs as humans, performing the same functions and controlled by the same mechanisms. It claims that differences between animals and humans could lead to exciting new developments. For example, a mouse with muscular dystrophy suffers less muscle wasting than a human patient. If we could find out why, we could discover a treatment for the disorder.

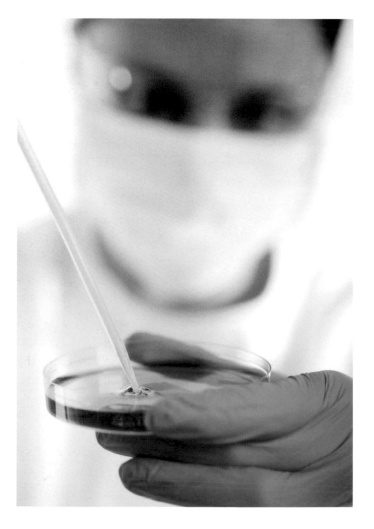

Some animal hormones have been used successfully in humans. They include insulin from the pancreas of pigs and cows and thyrotropin from the pituitary glands of cows. Charles Cornelius, a veterinary surgeon, has compiled a list of 350 animal diseases which are very similar to human diseases.

The evidence that the RDS uses to back up its case does not really address the issues. Instead, it says that after animal testing, any new drug is tested on 3-5,000 human volunteers, and that if any side effect shows up only after a drug has been put on the market, it cannot be blamed on animal testing. It says that there are 2,000 types of drug available in this country. Uncaged suggests there are 20,000, most of which are slight variations on a theme. The World Health Organisation has stated that there are just 268 drugs which are essential to human health. What are all the others?

RDS claims that less than 40 drugs have been withdrawn from the market because of adverse side effects in the UK, US, France and Germany since 1961, and of these, only 10 have been withdrawn in all four countries. Professor Croce however claims that from 1972 to June 1983, 22,621 medicinal preparations had their registrations revoked. He obtained his figures from the Italian Ministry of Health's Drug Information Bulletin. He also states that all of these potential medicines must have passed their animal test stage in order to have been granted a registration. It could be that Italian drug testing procedures are less stringent than English, American, French and German ones, but it seems likely that in these countries, many drugs pass their animal testing phase and only fail to be marketed because subsequent tests on humans reveal side effects not indicated by the animal tests. The number is likely to be in the thousands, as in Italy, but it is not in RDS's interest to report this, so we have no clear figure available. Clearly, there are different ways of telling the 'truth', which involve the statistics you choose to publish. They simply tell very different sides of the same story.

According to RDS, alternative testing methods, such as in vitro testing, computer modelling and studies of patients and population are already extensively used. In fact, it claims that only five pence in every pound spent on medical research goes on animal studies. It says that 'alternative' methods are not really alternatives at all. It believes that there are no alternatives to animal testing, as it is important to know how different systems within the body interact. Tests on animals are there to ensure that no obviously poisonous substances are tested on human volunteers. Professor Croce's evidence suggests that animal testing is not the safeguard that the RDS claims it is, and that very many new drugs, whilst not directly harmful, are also ineffective as cures.

Animal testing is used as a defence by the manufacturers not only of drugs, but of household cleaners and other everyday substances. If a product has been tested on animals, it

can be used as a defence if it causes harm to people. For example, in America, artificial sweeteners like Sweet 'N Low carry the warning "Use of this product may be hazardous to your health. This product contains saccharin which has been determined to cause cancer in laboratory animals." The laboratory animals in question were rats which were given saccharin in doses equivalent in human terms to 800 - 1000 cans of soft drink per day for life! Overdosing on anything is likely to produce serious harm or even death, so what does this kind of test prove? It turned out that male rats had a chemical in their bodies which caused the saccharin to crystalise in their bladders, irritating them and causing bladder cancers. Female rats were less likely to suffer the cancers, as they had less of the chemical in their bodies. However this test did nothing to show the potential dangers to humans, who do not have the same chemical present in their bodies anyway.

Other examples of highly unpleasant testing are the LD50, LD100 and Draize eye tests. LD50 is the test to show how much of a substance it takes to kill 50% of the animals being tested. LD100 finds the dosage level at which all the tested animals die. Needless to say, the 50% of animals which do not die in LD50 testing must suffer terribly from the effects of a substance which has killed the other 50%.

Clearly, many animal experiments are cruel and unnecessary, but there are also many examples of animal experimentation which have caused great advances in human medicine. Just one example is the case of diabetes. In 1889, two scientists, von Mering and Minkowski showed that removing a dog's pancreas produced diabetes. This showed for the first time that the pancreas was responsible for regulating blood sugar.

In 1921, two Canadian scientists, Banting and Best attempted to produce insulin and showed that giving insulin to a dog that had had its pancreas removed helped lower its blood sugar. Before long, James Collip, a biochemist, had extracted insulin from beef pancreas which was pure enough to be able to treat diabetic patients. He needed to find out what concentration of insulin to use, and used rabbits to carry out his tests. His extracts were used successfully in dogs and humans in 1922. The results were described by the British Medical Journal as "a magnificent contribution to the treatment of diabetes". In Britain today, there are around hundreds of thousands of diabetics who have to inject insulin and worldwide there could be as many as 30 million. A better advertisement for animal testing would be difficult to find.

In conclusion

Many animal experiments are cruel, painful, and seem unnecessary. Yet many of them are extremely beneficial to humans. In a country in which millions of animals are killed every week to feed and clothe us, can we really be too critical of experiments which may lead to exciting new discoveries? Is it fair to wave the finger at the vivisectionist from over our Sunday roast?

Clearly, there are some very bad vivisectionists who do not care about the suffering they are inflicting on the animals they experiment on. Indeed, it would be almost impossible to do the job of a vivisectionist if you cared too much about the animals you were performing experiments on.

However, exciting discoveries are still made by vivisectionists, which are beneficial to humans, and there are many people who are suffering from diseases and live in hope of a cure being found for them through animal testing.

Do animals need to be sacrificed in order to test new cosmetics? Don't we have enough cosmetic ingredients available already? Yet if you are buying cosmetics without checking whether they have been tested on animals, then you could be guilty of encouraging further tests to be carried out.

Better regulation of animal testing is clearly the key. The Animals (Scientific Procedures) Act 1986 is described by the Home Office as "widely viewed as the most rigorous piece of legislation of its type in the world." Yet it was still possible for over 40 hours of incriminating video-tape to be shot secretly by an animal rights activist in the laboratory of Professor Willhelm Feldberg, a researcher licenced by the Animal Procedures Committee.

The animal rights activists and vivisectionists should work together to ensure that only sensible, productive experiments are carried out. Steps should be taken to stop pharmaceutical companies from developing "copycat' medicines (ones which vary only slightly in formula from a successful drug already produced by another company).

You cannot say that all tests carried out on animals are wrong, especially if you eat meat or wear leather shoes and clothing but at the same time it is impossible to condone the many senseless, repetitive studies carried out on substances and medicines which we don't really need anyway.

25 December 2019

The above information is reprinted with kind permission from *The Young People's Trust for the Environment*. © YPTE 2020

www.ypte.org.uk

Animal testing: is it justified?

By Lily Holbrook

Throughout the history of scientific research, animal testing has revolutionised our understanding of psychological and physical health. However, this has not come without widespread ethical debate. Following the shocking news that Swedish researchers are to euthanise six Labradors in the name of science, can we justify harming animals for human benefit?

It is undeniable that we have learnt a lot about humans based on studies that have been conducted on animals. From the shocking effects of maternal deprivation shown to us by Harlow's monkeys in the 1950s, to the finding that neurotransmitter levels in the brain can alter emotional state following tests on rodents the decade later, we are becoming increasingly well-equipped to maximise human health through discoveries made by testing on animals.

While the latter of these examples may be justified by its important application in the development of anti-depressants, there are other experiments where the benefits to humans, and certainly to the animals involved, are less clear.

Some even appear to be needless, calling into question how far we can justify such practices. What about the 1950s Russian multi-dog experiment where the head of a puppy was surgically removed from its own body and attached alongside the head and body of an adult dog?

While we would hope that ethics standards have improved since then, research into dental implants currently being conducted by Swedish researchers at Gothenburg University has sparked a lot of controversy. Despite over 80,000 signatures opposing the medical trials, the final stage of the research will see the 6 dogs involved in the study euthanised for tissue analysis following experiments that included removal of their teeth.

As highlighted by the study above, the main issue with animal testing is undoubtedly the suffering caused without consent. However, in an advancing world of technology, it may now be possible to come up with viable alternatives that do not bring harm to animals. But what are they?

In vitro methods using cells and tissues

The Draize Test, developed in 1944, is a toxicology test involving a painful procedure where animals such as rabbits are directly used to measure the irritating effects of chemicals on the eye. However, the in vitro culture of bovine cornea, using cells rather than directly testing on the animal, may considerably reduce animal suffering while still effectively determining the toxicology of test chemicals.

Smaller organisms

Granted, this is still a form of animal testing. However, using smaller animals and bacterial organisms that take up less space and have a shorter life cycle are ideal for lab testing, and may replace larger animals such as rabbits and mice that we perceive to experience pain most akin to human suffering.

In silico methods using computer modelling

Living in a world increasingly dominated by a switch to computerised systems, virtual models of disease progression are in constant development to predict the effects of drugs. This may be achieved by quantitative structure-activity relationships (QSARs) which are computer-based techniques that can estimate the toxicity of a substance based on similarity to already known substances and our existing knowledge of human biology.

Human volunteers

It sounds simple, but small trials on human patients are vital for assessing the effect of drugs before they are made available to the wider population. Crucially, these tests can be used to eliminate drug compounds that are ineffective on humans before needless testing on animals.

Human simulators

Dissecting animals to understand human systems has been a part of education for decades. Now, human simulators which can breathe, talk and even bleed are being introduced to teach physiology in US medical schools which may pave the way for a future without needless animal exploitation.

Organs on chips

This one sounds very futuristic. But human cells grown on chips to replicate human physiology, diseases and drug responses are becoming a reality and may have applications in a number of scientific fields. Another bonus is that they are more accurate than animal responses, so may solve not only a major ethical debate, but also issues on whether or not findings from animal studies can be generalised to humans.

There is a huge spectrum where people stand on the issue of animal testing. Some people think it is acceptable to test on animals for medical purposes, but not cosmetic. But what about using animals for food, as pets or in sport? There is not one easy answer.

Animal testing undoubtedly has its benefits, but it also has an array of ethical drawbacks.

Regardless of the long-term benefit to humankind of animal research, the fact that animals do not have a voice in the human world is something we should consider when assuming they are ours to test upon.

24 February 2019

The above information is reprinted with kind permission from The Courier Online.
© 2020 The Courier Online

www.thecourieronline.co.uk

EU reports reveal catalogue of suffering: more than 20 million animals languished in laboratories

By Margarita S

New figures published by the European Commission reveal that cruel and archaic experiments are rampant across the EU. In 2017, 9.39 million mice, rats, fish, dogs, and other animals were used for the first time in cruel experiments and other scientific procedures.

The creation and breeding of animals with debilitating genetic modifications accounted for an additional 1.28 million individuals. The UK was the most prolific user of animals in the EU, using an appalling 2.51 million animals in laboratories.

Here are the top three offenders for authorising experiments on animals in the EU in 2017:

1 UK: 2.51 million animals

2 Germany: 2.03 million animals

3 France: 1.87 million animals

These shocking figures don't even include the 12.6 million animals who were used as breeding machines in the cruel supply chain or who languished in cages without being used for experiments. In 2017 in the UK alone, 1.81 million animals either were bred for laboratory use but didn't fit the 'right' criteria at the 'right' time or were killed so that their body parts could be used in experiments. Animals are often seen as nothing more than furry test tubes – disposed of like unfeeling, inanimate objects when they're no longer of any use to the experimenter.

What can be done to animals in EU laboratories?

As long as an experimenter fills out the right paperwork, there are very few limitations on the types of atrocities that can be inflicted on animals in laboratories. Here are just three routine examples:

Experimenters restrain dogs, rabbits, and guinea pigs and deliberately apply potentially toxic chemicals to their shaved skin or their eyes or force them down their throats. As a result, the animals may develop tumours, sustain burns, or go blind. If they survive until the end of the test, they are typically killed and their organs dissected.

Experimenters kill millions of fish for toxicity tests. Different concentrations of potentially toxic chemicals are added to tanks of water containing fish, causing them to gasp, tumble, and writhe in pain, and some eventually die.

In the forced swim test – once called the 'behavioural despair test' – experimenters put mice, rats, guinea pigs, hamsters, or gerbils in inescapable containers filled with water. The panicked animals try to escape by attempting to climb up the sides of the beakers or even diving underwater in search of an exit. They paddle furiously, desperately trying to keep their heads above water. Eventually, they start to float.

These cruel experiments are bad science. They can't reliably be used to predict what will happen in humans or to the environment, and attempting to do so can be dangerous.

Non-animal research methods are the future

As more and more evidence shows that results from tests on animals are rarely applicable to human conditions and diseases, we're seeing scientists, government agencies, and funding bodies shift their focus towards human-relevant, animal-free methods.

From techniques using human cells and tissues to computer simulations and organs-on-chips, animal-free science is providing the scientific revolution that's essential to protecting humans, the environment, and animals.

One of the most recent achievements in the UK is the closure of the Wellcome Sanger Institute animal testing facility, announced in May 2019. The institute is moving away from experimenting on animals and towards using cell-based methods.

Promising progress has been made in other countries, too. The Dutch government has committed to ending the use of animals for toxicity testing by 2025, and in 2019, the US Environmental Protection Agency (EPA) announced plans to stop funding and requesting tests on mammals by 2035. PETA US first put animal rights on the EPA's agenda 20 years ago, and while we wish animal tests would stop now – or had never started – this is the first time a US regulatory agency has made such a commitment.

For institutions to stick to these admirable commitments, significantly more resources must be devoted to the development and adoption of animal-free methods.

What next?

We're calling for the UK government to commit to phasing out all experiments on animals and redirecting resources towards superior, non-animal tests. Now that the UK has withdrawn from the European Union, it's essential that our leaders consider the implications for animals in laboratories. For example, we may see a sharp increase in the duplication of cruel tests on animals for separate EU and UK legislation.

The UK must justify its reputation as a nation of animal lovers and establish a strategy to end experiments on animals.

5 February 2020

The above information is reprinted with kind permission from PETA.
© 2020 PETA

www.peta.org.uk

Annual Statistics of Scientific Procedures on Living Animals, Great Britain, 2019

Key results

 **-3%**

In 2019, 3.40 million procedures were carried out in Great Britain involving living animals. This is a decrease of 3% on last year, and the lowest number of procedures since 2007.

 **51%**

Around half of all procedures were experimental procedures (1.73 million), whilst the other half were for the creation and breeding of genetically altered (GA) animals (1.67 million).

93%

The majority (93%) of procedures (both for experimental and breeding purposes) used mice, fish or rats. These species have been the most used for the past decade.

 **57%**

Over half (57%) of experimental procedures were for the purpose of basic research, most commonly focusing on the the immune system, the nervous system and cancer.

Source: Annual Statistics of Scientific Procedures on Living Animals, Great Britain, 2019

Summary statistics

3.40 million procedures were carried out in Great Britain involving living animals in 2019

 Experimental procedures

1.73 million procedures carried out for experimental purposes

These procedures involve using animals in scientific studies for purposes such as: basic research and the development of treatments, safety testing of pharmaceuticals and other substances, specific surgical training and education, environmental research and species protection.

 Creation and breeding of GA animals

1.67 million procedures for the creation and breeding of GA animals.

This refers to the breeding of animals whose genes have mutated or have been modified. These animals are used to produce GA offspring for use in experimental procedures but are not themselves used in experimental procedures.

Species

 61% of procedures used mice

 16% of procedures used fish

9% of procedures used rats

 87% were for creation/breeding of mice

 12% were for creation/breeding of fish

 1% were for creation/breeding of rats

Purpose of procedures

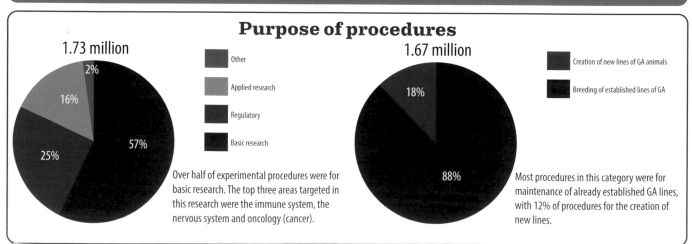

1.73 million

- Other — 2%
- Applied research — 16%
- Regulatory — 25%
- Basic research — 57%

Over half of experimental procedures were for basic research. The top three areas targeted in this research were the immune system, the nervous system and oncology (cancer).

1.67 million

- Creation of new lines of GA animals — 18% / 12%
- Breeding of established lines of GA — 88%

Most procedures in this category were for maintenance of already established GA lines, with 12% of procedures for the creation of new lines.

Source: Annual Statistics of Scientific Procedures on Living Animals, Great Britain, 2019

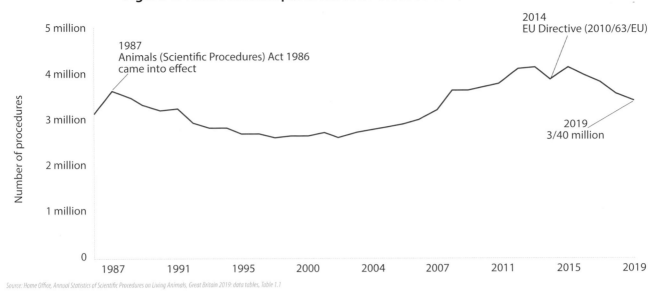

Figure 1. Total scientific procedures in Great Britain, 1986 to 2019

1987
Animals (Scientific Procedures) Act 1986 came into effect

2014
EU Directive (2010/63/EU)

2019
3/40 million

Source: Home Office, Annual Statistics of Scientific Procedures on Living Animals, Great Britain 2019: data tables, Table 1.1

Total procedures

Key results

♦ In 2019, there were 3.40 million procedures completed on living animals in Great Britain. This is a decrease of 3% from last year, and the lowest number of procedures since 2007.

♦ Procedures for creation and breeding have decreased by 3% and experimental procedures have decreased by 4%.

As shown in Figure 1, the number of procedures carried out decreased from 1987 until 2001, to a low of 2.62 million. This was mainly due to a reduction in the use of rodents, rabbits and birds (although there was an increase in procedures involving fish).

After 2001, procedures increased, reaching a peak of 4.14 million in 2015, but has decreased since to 3.40 million in 2019. This is the lowest number of procedures carried out in a single year since 2007.

The number of procedures carried out on living animals is determined by several factors, including the focus of scientific and medical endeavours, the economic climate and global trends in new technologies or fields of research.

Experimental procedures

Key results

♦ Of the 1.73 million experimental procedures, the majority (86%; 1.49 million) used mice, fish or rats.

♦ Over half (57%) of all experimental procedures were carried out for basic research purposes (984,000 procedures). The most common areas focused on in this research were: the immune system (21%), the nervous system (21%) and cancer (oncology;15%).

♦ In 2019, 91% of all experimental procedures were assessed as sub-threshold, mild or moderate in severity, the remainder were non-recovery or severe.

Species

The proportions of species used for experimental procedures as shown in Figure 3 have remained mostly stable for the past decade.

For most species, small year-on-year variations can be attributed to technological developments and changes in the types and stages of projects being carried out in any reporting year.

Purpose

Experimental procedures accounted for half (51%) of the 3.40 million procedures in 2019. Figure 7 shows the purpose of these procedures.

As shown in Figure 7, over half (57%) of the experimental procedures carried out in 2019 were for basic research. A

Figure 3. Experimental procedures by species, 2019

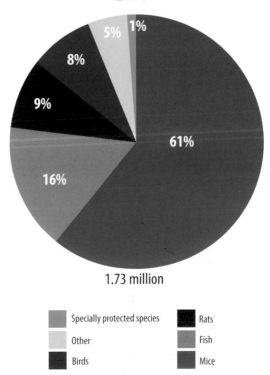

1.73 million

▨ Specially protected species		■ Rats
▨ Other		▨ Fish
■ Birds		■ Mice

Source: Home Office, Annual Statistics of Scientific Procedures on Living Animals, Great Britain 2019: data tables, Table 1.2
Notes: Specially protected species are Cats, Dogs, Horses and Primates.

Figure 7. Experimental procedures by purpose, 2019

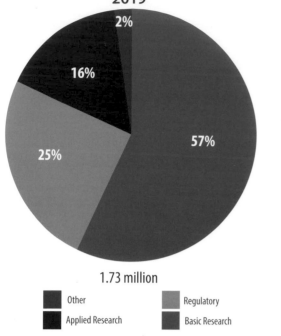

1.73 million

- Other
- Applied Research
- Regulatory
- Basic Research

Source: Home Office, Annual Statistics of Scientific Procedures on Living Animals, Great Britain 2019: data tables, Table 1.2
Notes: Experimental procedures carried out for higher education or training, the preservation of species and for the protection of the national environment accounted for 2% and therefore are not visible.

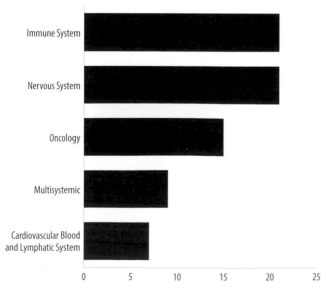

Figure 8. Most common areas focused upon in experimental procedures for basic research, 2019

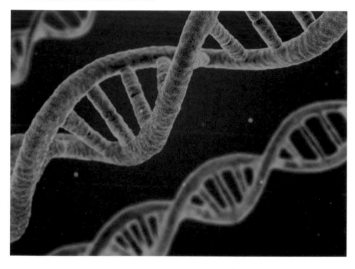

- Immune System
- Nervous System
- Oncology
- Multisystemic
- Cardiovascular Blood and Lymphatic System

0 5 10 15 20 25

Source: Home Office, Annual Statistics of Scientific Procedures on Living Animals, Great Britain 2019: data tables, Table 5
Notes: Research is classified as multisystemic when numerous body organs and systems are targeted

Basic research:

aims to expand our knowledge of the structure, functioning and behaviour of living organisms and the environment.

Applied research:

attempts to address diseases through prevention and development of treatments. Within the data tables, this is shown as 'Translational/Applied research'.

Regulatory testing:

procedures carried out to satisfy legal requirements, including: ensuring substances are produced to legal specification; evaluating the safety or effectiveness of pharmaceuticals and other substances.

further 25% were conducted for regulatory testing purposes, and the remainder were mostly for applied research (16%).

Basic research

In 2019, 984,000 experimental procedures were carried out for basic research purposes. The most common areas focused upon in this research, as shown in Figure 8, were: the nervous system (21%), the immune system (21%), and cancer (oncology; 15%).

Creation and breeding of genetically altered animals

Key results

♦ Almost all (over 99%) of the 1.67 million procedures for the creation and breeding of GA animals involved mice, fish and rats.

♦ Most procedures counted under creation and breeding (88%) were for the maintenance of already established GA lines.

♦ The majority (74%) of procedures for creation and breeding in 2019 were assessed as sub-threshold in severity.

Species

Almost all (over 99%) of the procedures for the creation and breeding of GA animals involved mice (87%), fish (12%) or rats (0.5%). Other species used for creation and breeding of GA animals include: amphibians, ungulates (including pigs), and birds – but together they accounted for 0.2% of these procedures.

No specially protected species (horses, dogs, cats or primates) were used in procedures counted under creation and breeding of GA animals.

Genetic status

Of the 1.67 million procedures for creation and breeding that used GA animals in 2019, the majority (83%) used GA animals with no harmful phenotype (i.e. the animals did not appear or behave any differently from non-GA animals).

Figure 13. Creation and breeding of GA animals by type of genetic alteration, 2015 to 2019

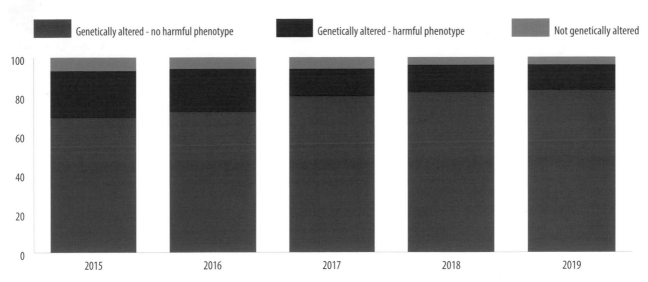

Source: Home Office, Annual Statistics of Scientific Procedures on Living Animals, Great Britain 2019: data tables, Table 8

As shown in Figure 13, there has been an increase in proportion of animals used for creation and breeding that are genetically altered without a harmful phenotype (rising from 70% of all creation and breeding in 2015 to 83% in 2019).

There were some animals that were bred with the intention of producing GA animals, but resulted in non-GA animals being born (4% of animals in this category in 2019). In addition, some animals used for the creation of a new genetic line will also have been genetically normal animals (e.g. those used for superovulation).

Purpose

As shown in Figure 14, of the total 1.67 million procedures for the creation and breeding of GA animals, 88% were for the maintenance of already established GA lines, with the remainder of procedures for the creation of new lines.

Of the 197,000 procedures that were for the creation of new GA lines, almost all (94%) were to create new GA lines to be used in basic research. More specifically, these animals were bred to be used in procedures focusing on multisystemic

research (39,000 breeding procedures), the immune system (39,000 breeding procedures), and nervous system (31,000 breeding procedures).

16 July 2020

Figure 14. Creation and breeding of GA animals by purpose, 2019

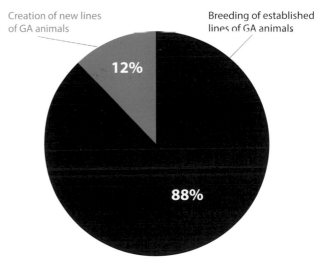

Source: Home Office, Annual Statistics of Scientific Procedures on Living Animals, Great Britain 2019: data tables, Tables 8, 9.1 and 10

Creation:

includes the natural breeding of different strains to produce a new strain and procedures that use standard techniques such as vasectomy for the generation of novel transgenic or mutant lines of GA animals. The birth of a GA animal counts as creation when the line is new and before is it 'established' (i.e. stable and characterised).

Breeding:

the production of GA animals of an established line that has been bred for at least two generations. Breeding procedures also include other techniques applied to the animal after birth e.g. genotyping but not any techniques applied as part of an experiment or study.

The above information is reprinted with kind permission from The Home Office.
© Crown copyright 2020
This information is licensed under the Open Government Licence v3.0
To view this licence, visit http://www.nationalarchives.gov.uk/doc/open-government-licence/ **OGL**

www.gov.uk

The show can't go on: the fight for an EU-wide ban on wild animals in circuses

Four ex-circus lions discovered in France are due to be re-housed at Born Free, invigorating the call for an EU-wide ban on wild animals in circuses.

By Jacob Dykes

Whip-wielding, top-hat-wearing lion tamers may seem anachronistic, yet the exploitation of wild animals in circuses continues today. A French circus owner was recently attacked by one of his lions, prompting the surrender of four cats to the authorities. Angela, Bellone, Louga and Saïda will be re-housed at Born Free's sanctuary at Shamwari Private Game Reserve in South Africa.

Dr Chris Draper, head of animal welfare and captivity at Born Free, has seen the conditions of European circuses first hand. 'Conditions are woefully inadequate. Animals are made to perform once or twice a day. They're living cheek by jowl, often with predator and prey side-by-side.'

Thirty-one countries worldwide and 18 EU countries have banned the use of wild animals in circuses; 24 EU countries restrict the use of animals in one form or another. However, in the absence of EU-wide legislation, circuses have exploited regional and national differences in enforcement. Several EU countries have only restrictions on the use of wild animals in place, not bans. Some, including France, Germany, and Lithuania, are yet to adopt any restrictions. In Spain, murky legislative waters are enforced at the municipality or regional level – more Spanish municipalities are banning wild animals in circuses, but a nationwide ban is yet to come into effect.

As travelling performances, circuses can simply move to regions where wild animals are still permitted to perform. EU member states which have banned the use of wild animals are obliged to allow travelling circuses to move through their territory. Ilaria Di Silvestre, programme leader for wildlife at Eurogroup for Animals, thinks that the absence of an EU-wide ban exacerbates poor conditions: 'They are spending even longer on the road, crossing Europe to reach areas where they're still allowed to perform.'

According to a YouGov 2018 opinion poll conducted for the NGO Animal Advocacy and Protection, 65 per cent of Europeans condemn the use of wild animals in circuses. 'Polls have shown that it's not really a problem of public support, it's getting the politicians to understand that [wild animals in circuses] should be a priority. EU-level politicians and the European Commission say that it's the responsibility of member states to enforce,' says Di Silvestre.

Organisations such as Born Free, Eurogroup for Animals and InfoCircos are promulgating the need for EU-wide regulation to address the problem. 'In my experience, the only effective stance is a blanket ban on the use of wild animals in circuses. Any sort of halfway house is open to abuse,' says Draper. With an estimated 500 to 1,500 wild animals in French circuses alone, many experts have called for an interim,

Legislation of European Union Member States on the use of animals in circuses: EU Member States enforce divergent legislation on the use of animals in circuses, leaving grey areas open to exploitation. France, Germany, Italy and Lithuania are yet to adopt any restrictions

Source: Geographical

Legend:
- National ban on all animals
- National ban on wild animals
- Regional bans of wild animals
- Legal restrictions on use of wild animals
- No restrictions on use of wild animals

transition period to precede a blanket ban in the EU, in which sanctuaries for wildlife can be bolstered to habilitate the influx of newly-protected animals. 'Governments don't fully know what animals are out there. We'd need to identify the animals currently in circuses, prevent new ones coming in, both from breeding or trade, and ensure each animal is identifiable through micro-chipping: it's got to be strategic, and it's got to be entirely humane,' adds Draper.

Circuses are supposed to comply with EU Council Regulation 338/97, protecting endangered species of wild fauna and flora by restricting their trade. However, Draper is sceptical that circuses can remain financially viable through performances alone. 'Lions and tigers will continue to breed even in the worst facilities, so there's a never-ending supply of cubs. I'm curious about how circuses are staying afloat – there is a strong suspicion that some are breeding and selling cubs into the exotic pet trade to supplement their income.'

The inclusion of wild animals in legal circuses may therefore be perpetuating the commodification of dangerous and endangered species.

Di Silvestre is hopeful that the tides are turning. The French government is currently reviewing its legislation on wild animals in circuses, Italy is drafting new legislation, and a petition calling for an EU-wide ban, led by InfoCircos, has drawn just under one million signatures. However, it is clear that until an EU-wide ban is enforced, circus owners will continue to exploit grey areas in legislation, and prolong the exploitation of wild animals.

22 June 2020

The above information is reprinted with kind permission from Geographical.
© 2020 Syon Geographical Ltd

www.geographical.co.uk

UXBRIDGE COLLEGE
LEARNING CENTRE

Lucy's Law: third-party puppy sales banned as new law comes into force

Government urges public to help ensure new law is a success.

By Tom Bawden

The RSPCA has warned that Covid-19 could have a huge impact on the welfare of newborn puppies as the Lucy's Law ban on third-party sales comes into force.

The association welcomed the new law, which means that from Monday, all dogs must now be bought from the breeder, or from a reputable rescue organisation.

However, it expressed concern that just as the law was being brought in, puppy welfare faces a major threat from coronavirus.

'We have concerns that the Covid-19 lockdown will have a huge impact on animal welfare in this area,' said David Bowles, of the RSPCA.

'Many puppies who have been bred to sell in time for the summer boom will be left languishing and suffering in silence in terrible conditions on puppy farms, or will be abandoned and left to fend for themselves.'

The RSPCA revealed that it has looked into almost 28,168 complaints about the illegal puppy trade in the last 10 years.

The law is named after Lucy, a Cavalier King Charles Spaniel who was rescued from a puppy farm where she was subjected to terrible conditions.

Puppy farms are located across the UK with most depending on third-party sellers or 'dealers' to distribute often sick, traumatised, unsocialised puppies which have been taken away from their mother at just a few weeks old.

This often involves long-distance transportation, with the puppy or kitten suffering life-threatening medical, surgical, or behavioural problems which are passed on to unsuspecting new owners.

What is Lucy's Law?

Lucy's Law effectively removes the third-party dealer chain, resulting in all dog and cat breeders becoming accountable for the first time, according to the government.

Animal welfare minister Lord Goldsmith said: 'Today is a significant milestone for animal welfare, and a major step towards ending cruel puppy farming and smuggling.

'But we also need the public to do their bit to help by always asking to see puppies and kittens interacting with their mothers in their place of birth, looking out for the warning signs, and reporting any suspicious activity.'

He added: 'By raising awareness of illegal sellers to the local authorities, we can all help to protect the nation's cats and dogs and give them the best start in life.'

6 April 2020

The above information is reprinted with kind permission from *iNews*.
© 2020 JPIMedia Ltd.

www.inews.co.uk

Does trophy hunting help conservation?

A new Born Free report is busting the myths and exposing the cruelty behind trophy hunting, starting with the claim that it can actually benefit wildlife conservation.

Every year, hundreds of thousands of animals, including threatened species, are targeted by trophy hunters who pay large sums of money to hunt, kill and export body parts back home, to be displayed as trophies.

Hunters often claim the fees they pay to government agencies, hunting outfitters, taxidermists and shipping companies in order to secure and export their trophy benefit local communities on the ground, and the economies of the countries where trophy hunting takes place.

Many also claim that wildlife itself benefits from trophy hunting because only problem or redundant animals are targeted, and so the practice is a legitimate form of population control.

Against a backdrop of increasing public outcry in response to individual cases such as Cecil the lion, Born Free's report explains why the hunters' conservation claims are drastically missing the mark.

Dr Mark Jones, Born Free's Head of Policy, says: 'Claims by trophy hunters that they are primarily concerned about wildlife conservation or animal management are highly

10 facts about trophy hunting

Trophy hunting is the killing of an animal for sport or pleasure in order to display part or all of its body as a trophy.

Born Free is opposed to the killing of any animal for sport or pleasure and is against all forms of trophy hunting. One of our working priorities is to eliminate trophy hunting by exposing its fundamental immorality and demonstrating alternative solutions.

According to the Convention on International Trade in Endangered Species (CITES), 290,000 trophy items from nearly 300 CITES-listed species were exported across the world between 2008 and 2017.

The top five exporting countries for those trophy items were South Africa, Canada, Mozambique, Namibia and Zimbabwe.

The top five destination countries were the United States, South Africa, Singapore, Germany and Spain.

The top five species were the Nile crocodile, American black bear, African elephant, hippopotamus and zebra.

Trophy hunting does not benefit wildlife conservation. Hunting proponents often claim the money generated through hunting fees goes towards funding wildlife conservation agencies, and that hunters can help control wildlife populations by removing problem or redundant individuals. However, little of the money generated through trophy hunting goes back into conservation. Rather than targeting problem or redundant animals, trophy hunters tend to covet animals with particular traits which make them good trophies. The killing of these individuals can have serious adverse consequences, which can threaten future population health and viability.

Local communities rarely benefit from trophy hunting. An analysis by economists of data produced by the International Council for Game and Wildlife Conservation and the UN Food and Agriculture Organisation, found that hunting companies contribute on average just 3% of their revenues to communities living in hunting areas. The vast majority of their income goes to government agencies, outfitters and individuals located in national capitals and overseas.

Trophy hunting does not benefit the local economy to any significant degree. A 2017 study concluded that "the current total economic contribution of trophy hunters from their hunting-related, and non-hunting related, tourism is about 0.03% of GDP". In contrast, a study found a live elephant may be worth as much as $1.6m over its lifetime through income from photographic tourism – many times the fee typically paid by a trophy hunter to shoot an elephant.

Trophy hunting does not consider animal welfare. Hunters may not be expert shots, and are encouraged to use weapons such as bows and arrows, handguns or muzzle-loaders – the use of which increases the likelihood of animals being wounded and suffering. Target animals may be pursued for long periods of time during hunts. Individuals may be separated from family groups or populations, which may result in considerable stress.

misleading. Trophy hunters don't target problem or surplus animals; instead they covet those animals with the most impressive traits – the largest tusks, or the darkest manes. By doing so they remove key individuals, severely disrupting animal families and populations. They also cause immense animal suffering. Trophy hunting is not a conservation or animal management tool, nor does it contribute significant funds to conservation programmes or local communities; it is a cruel relic from colonial times that should be consigned to history where it belongs.'

Trophy hunters value rarity, and in some cases are prepared to pay large amounts of money to kill very rare animals, which means that these species may be disproportionately targeted, and may be driven towards extinction as a result. A recent report prepared for the International Union for the Conservation of Nature and others, noted that 40% of the big game hunting zones in Zambia and 72% in Tanzania are now classified as depleted, because the big game has been hunted out of these areas.

Dr Jones added: 'Recent attempts in Zambia to justify the trophy hunting of up to 1,250 hippos in the Luangwa Valley using claims of overpopulation and disease risk, show how cynical authorities and hunting proponents can be. The hunts had nothing to do with animal management, and were clearly designed to line the pockets of a few individuals and hunting outfitters. Thanks to local and international pressure, those plans have been abandoned. We need to challenge trophy hunting wherever it takes place.'

Born Free is opposed to the killing of any animal for sport or pleasure and is against all forms of trophy hunting. One of our working priorities is to eliminate trophy hunting by exposing its fundamental immorality and demonstrating that wildlife can be conserved and managed humanely.

The above information is reprinted with kind permission from the Born Free Foundation.
© 2020 Born Free Foundation

www.bornfree.org.uk

29

YouGov poll reveals vast majority (93%) of Brits don't wear real animal fur and do support a #FurFreeBritain; Government urged to end UK fur sales

Dame Judi Dench, Ricky Gervais, Leona Lewis support #FurFreeBritain campaign for UK fur sales ban.

British citizens overwhelmingly agree that the time has come for Britain to be fur-free. A new YouGov opinion poll, commissioned by animal charity Humane Society International/UK, reveals that 93% of the British population reject wearing real animal fur, and the majority (72%) support a complete ban on the sale of fur in the UK. The poll also demonstrates Brits' scathing view of fur – the words that people most closely associate with a fashion brand selling fur are 'unethical', 'outdated', 'cruel' and 'out of touch'.

HSI/UK released the poll as part of its #FurFreeBritain campaign for a UK fur sales ban, just one day after HSI's latest investigation exposed horrific suffering of foxes and raccoon dogs on fur farms in Asia.

HSI/UK's call for a fur sales ban addresses a double-standard left over from the year 2000's victory for animals, when the UK announced a ban on fur farming in Britain. However, the ban didn't prevent the import and sale of fur from animals farmed overseas, and since the ban came into effect in 2003, almost £800m of fur has been imported into the UK from fur farms in France, Italy, Poland, China and other countries. In 2018 almost £75m of animal fur was imported into the UK.

Claire Bass, executive director of Humane Society International/UK, said: 'This new poll shows without a doubt that most Brits reject fur, and they want that reflected in British law with a UK fur sales ban. Like us, they believe that if fur is too cruel to farm in the UK, it is too cruel to sell here too. The vast majority of designers and retailers have already turned their backs on outdated fur, so now it's time for the UK governments to take action. For as long as fur is sold in our shops, Britain is complicit in the suffering and death of millions of fur bearing animals for the fashion industry. British consumers have made their views clear – fur is cruel, outdated and it should be banned.'

YouGov/HSI poll results

The most significant statistics include:

♦ 72% support a ban on the import and sale of animal fur in the UK (rising to 81% of Scottish voters);

♦ the public most closely associate negative words, including 'unethical', 'cruel', 'outdated' and 'out of touch' with a fashion brand that sells real animal fur;

Fur facts

More than 100 million animals are killed for their fur every year worldwide including mink, fox, raccoon dog, chinchilla and coyote – that's equal to three animals dying every second, just for their fur.

Rabbits are also killed for their fur, likely to be in the hundreds of millions.

Fur comes with a hefty environmental price tag. Whilst all materials have some eco-footprint, when compared to other textiles, fur takes a significant toll in terms of the CO_2 emissions associated with keeping and feeding tens of thousands of carnivorous animals on a farm, the manure runoff into lakes and rivers, and the cocktail of toxic and carcinogenic chemicals such as chromium and formaldehyde used to preserve the fur and skin to stop it from rotting.

An increasing number of fashion designers and retailers are dropping fur cruelty. In the last few years alone Prada, Gucci, Armani, Versace, Michael Kors, Jimmy Choo, DKNY, Burberry, Chanel and other high-profile brands have announced fur-free policies. In addition, online fashion retail platforms Net-A-Porter and Farfetch have introduced no-fur policies.

- the vast majority of Brits reject wearing real fur: 83% have never worn real fur and another 10% have worn fur in the past but no longer do so. Only 3% currently wear real animal fur.

Bass continued, 'Any fashion brands or designers currently on the fence about whether or not to sell animal fur should take a close look at these poll results from a business perspective. When given free choice of a range of positive and negative words to describe a fashion brand that sells fur, 79% of people chose negative associations – unethical, cruel, outdated and out of touch. The fur trade's PR spin has failed to shake solid public perceptions that this is an industry that has no place in modern fashion.'

The #FurFreeBritain campaign has received support from a cross party group of MPs, and Early Day Motion 267, urging the government to introduce legislation banning the import and sale of real fur products, has so far been signed by 106 MPs, including Tracey Crouch, Maria Eagle, Dr Lisa Cameron and Tim Farron.

Celebrities have also expressed their shock at the animal suffering for the fur trade, and pledged their support for HSI's #FurFreeBritain campaign.

Dame Judi Dench said: '*I am proud that the UK was the first country in the world to ban fur farming, and I hope we will be*

Which of the following words would you most closely associate with a fashion brand that sells real animal fur? (percentage)	
Unethical	27
Cruel	24
Outdated	15
Out of touch	13
Luxury	6
Modern	1
Sustainable	0
On trend	0
None of the above	4
Don't know	10

the first country in the world to ban fur sales. Fur farming is cruel and unnecessary.'

Leona Lewis said: '*I love all animals, and believe they should be treated with kindness and respect. So as an animal lover I would never wear fur. That's why I'm a proud supporter of HSI's #FurFreeBritain campaign for a UK fur sales ban.'*

Ricky Gervais said: '*I will never understand why anyone would want to wear fur – a beautiful fox who has been beaten or electrocuted, a mink who has been gassed to death, or a coyote who has suffered in a leg hold trap and then been shot in the head. How can anyone want to wear that on their hat or their coat, and how can Britain still sell fur when we banned fur farming for being cruel? It's utter hypocrisy and that's why I wholeheartedly support HSI's #FurFreeBritain campaign.'*

HSI/UK's most recent investigation of fur farms in Asia shows foxes and raccoon dogs living miserable lives in appalling conditions, and enduring painful deaths. Foxes were filmed being repeatedly bludgeoned over the head, resulting in catastrophic injury but not instant death in many cases, and other animals were kicked and cut with knives, or even skinned alive.

9 July 2020

The above information is reprinted with kind permission from Humane Society International.
© 2020 Humane Society International

www.hsi.org

Is your fake fur actually real? Here's how to tell the difference

Real animal fur can be produced and sold cheaply and is often less expensive for suppliers to use than synthetic alternatives.

By Katie Grant

Leaving the house in a mink coat and raccoon-fur trimmed gloves would once have guaranteed envious glances and a string of compliments, yet today such sartorial choices would be more likely to provoke dirty looks and disdainful comments.

Consumers – including those able to afford the real thing – have turned to the faux alternative in their masses over the past decade.

However, in recent years it has emerged that multiple retailers have been unknowingly selling items containing real fur masquerading as fake.

Online fashion retailer Boohoo is the latest to have been caught out – and not for the first time – by the animal welfare organisation Humane Society International. This week the Advertising Standards Authority announced Boohoo had broken rules by selling a jumper with 'faux' fur pom poms that were actually real.

The incident highlights how difficult it can be to ensure your clothes and accessories really are fur-free, and that labels often cannot be trusted.

Why would suppliers use real fur instead of fake?

Real fur can be produced and sold cheaply and is often less expensive for suppliers to use than synthetic alternatives, meaning many accessories and embellishments such as bobble hats, fluffy key rings and trims on parkas and hooded coats can actually be made from the real thing.

Here's how you can determine if a product features real or fake fur, according to the animal welfare body Humane Society International UK:

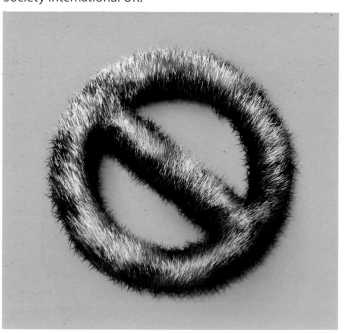

Check the ends of the fur

Real fur tends to taper to a point at the end of each strand, whereas the tip of faux fur tends to be blunt where it has been cut in the manufacturing process.

This is not the case 100 per cent of the time because any real fur that has been sheared will not be tapered, but this is the exception, not the rule.

Check the base of the fur

Part the hairs at the very base of the fur.

Faux fur will be attached to a fabric backing, identified by its weave look.

At the base of real fur, there will be an animal's skin (leather).

The burn test

You can't do this test in store obviously, but if you already own the item, then simply cutting off and carefully burning a few hairs will reveal whether the fur is real or fake.

If it's real animal fur, it will singe and smell like burnt human hair, whereas if it's fake, it will melt and curl into tiny balls, and smell like burnt plastic.

HSI UK stresses that burn tests should only be conducted in a safe environment, and on a small sample cut from the main item.

Labels can lie

It's not uncommon for the label on items, or the on-screen description if sold online, to give misleading information – so don't rely on them.

HSI UK has found numerous examples of items described as faux fur, or as comprising acrylic/synthetic, when in fact they are mislabelled real animal fur.

Shoes or non-garment accessories such as handbags and pom-pom keychains that contain fur don't have to carry any labelling at all.

The price is not right

Many consumers assume that if the price tag is cheap, it's unlikely to be real fur.

But the truth is that overheads on fur farms are so low that real fur trim can be bought by manufacturers for the same price or less than faux fur.

17 July 2020

The above information is reprinted with kind permission from *iNews*.
© 2020 JPIMedia Ltd.

www.inews.co.uk

Animal cruelty rampant in zoos with dolphins used as surfboards and elephants playing basketball

What might be seen as an enjoyable activity means a lifetime of suffering for these animals.

By Phoebe Weston

Cruelty is still rampant in the world's 'top' zoos according to new research which has found animals are being forced to learn tricks that would result in a 'lifetime of suffering'.

In a dozen zoos, big cats were still being forced to perform in gladiator-style shows in large amphitheatres, dolphins were still being used like surfboards and elephants were made to play basketball.

Researchers from the World Animal Protection and Change for Animals Foundation also say some zoos still clothe chimps in nappies and get them to drive around on scooters.

According to Dr Neil D'Cruze, Global Wildlife Advisor at World Animal Protection, all of these activities would have required cruel techniques to train these animals.

He said: 'Seeing wild animals perform in circus-like shows is not just a bit of fun. For the animals in these 12 irresponsible zoos, and potentially many others globally, what might be seen as an enjoyable activity on a day out for the family means a lifetime of suffering for these animals.

'Cruel and demeaning visitor attractions simply have no place in any modern leading zoo or aquarium.'

The global study involved investigating zoos and aquariums that are members of the World Association of Zoos and Aquariums (WAZA). The organisation was set up to encourage and support good standards of animal care and welfare.

They found out of WAZA's 1,200 venues, 75 per cent of them had at least one practice that researchers considered seriously detrimental to the animal's wellbeing.

Harry Eckman, the director of the Change for Animals Foundation, said: 'All of these ridiculous activities represent a clear and present danger to the wild animals involved.

'Circus-like shows and elephant rides typically involve harsh training methods to establish dominance and the use of wild animals as photo props can inflict stress and injuries.'

Researchers say visitors should reconsider visiting zoos where irresponsible practices are taking place.

Audrey Mealia, the group head of wildlife for World Animal Protection, said: 'Tourists visiting a WAZA-linked venue

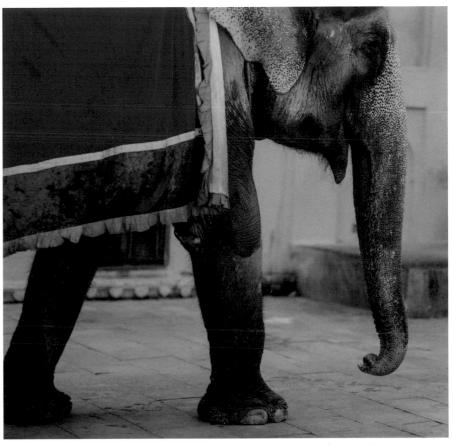

should be able to trust they are not inadvertently supporting cruel animal attractions. Sadly, currently this is not the case.'

Earlier this year an emaciated baby elephant was found forcing to bang her head to rave music and perform tricks under the threat of painful punishment at a Thai zoo, investigators found.

Behind-the-scenes footage showed the young animal chained up and repeatedly sucking on her trunk – a sign of distress – when away from the tourist shows.

The infant elephant, dubbed 'a real-life Dumbo', was made to join 'distressing' performances up to three times a day at Phuket Zoo. The investigators, from activist group Moving Animals, revealed that just after one month after their petition to save Dumbo launched the three-year-old elephant died after suffering from a digestive tract infection that had been undiagnosed for months.

29 July 2019

The above information is reprinted with kind permission from *The Independent*.
© independent.co.uk 2020

www.independent.co.uk

Should zoos still exist?

I'll start by saying that personally I'm fundamentally against zoos but I do understand some of the arguments why they should exist. My main reason for being against zoos is because I don't agree with caging animals for our entertainment.

I've disliked zoos since I was a small child. The memory of a polar bear pacing back and forth in a very small enclosure in a Yorkshire zoo has stuck with me. Many zoos now provide more space for their wild animals but it could hardly be described as equivalent to what they have in the wild. Keeping animals in climates that are not suited to them seems even more cruel.

Why zoos should exist

Bearing all of the above in mind, some zoos do actually carry out important conservation work. The arguments for zoos are many and varied…

The arguments for zoos

♦ Zoos can help to save endangered species by keeping them in a 'safe' environment. Safe as in protected from poachers, predators, habitat loss and even starvation.

♦ If a zoo has a breeding programme, this is another way to protect endangered species which may have trouble finding suitable mates in the wild.

♦ Zoos have an educational aspect. It's easier to learn about an animal by seeing them in person.

♦ Fostering empathy… By seeing an animal up close, the public might be encouraged to be more empathetic to a species that is facing extinction in the wild. They might put 2 and 2 together and realise the orangutan they saw is in jeopardy due to the products they buy (read about Palm Oil here).

♦ Good zoos have high standards of welfare for their animals. Visiting an accredited zoo is better than visiting one which isn't. For example, The Association of Zoos and Aquariums 'are leaders in the protection of threatened and endangered species.'

♦ A few zoos take in abandoned exotic pets and rehabilitate wildlife.

♦ Zoos are a traditional family activity.

Who are The Association of Zoos and Aquariums?

'The Association of Zoos and Aquariums (AZA) is a 501(c)3 non-profit organization dedicated to the advancement of zoos and aquariums in the areas of conservation, education, science and recreation. AZA represents more than 230 facilities in the United States and overseas, which collectively draw more than 200 million visitors every year. AZA-accredited zoos and aquariums meet the highest standards in animal care and welfare and provide a fun, safe, and educational family experience. In addition, they dedicate millions of dollars annually to support scientific research, conservation and education programs.'

Why zoos shouldn't exist

Just like there are quite a few arguments for the existence of zoos, whether you agree with them or not, there are also a lot of, if not many more, arguments against zoos.

The arguments against zoos

♦ Like the polar bear that's haunted me for over 35 years, animals in captivity often suffer from boredom and stress. Captivity can in no way compare to being free in the wild.

♦ What gives humans the right to capture, confine or breed other species? If an animal is endangered does that justify us removing its freedom?

♦ Most captive breeding programmes don't release animals into the wild. More often than not they become part of a never-ending chain of zoos, safari parks, circuses, canned hunting facilities and even the exotic pet trade. There are more tigers in American backyards than there are in the wild!

♦ Baby animals bring the visitors in in droves, but this often leads to zoos having too many animals. Surplus animals can be sold onto other zoos (or safari parks, circuses etc.) but many are just killed. You might remember back in 2014 when the Copenhagen Zoo in Denmark killed Marius the giraffe. 'Marius was dissected in front of a public audience, including children, and then fed to the zoo's lions.'

♦ Bonds between animals are broken when they are sold to alternative facilities which exploit animals, causing further stress to them.

♦ The wild populations of different endangered species may become less genetically diverse due to the removal of individuals from the wild, causing them to become even more endangered.

♦ If you want to see wild animals behaving normally they should be seen in the wild. Watching a dolphin performing tricks at Sea World in no way compares to a dolphin naturally jumping out of the water in the ocean.

♦ If you can't afford to see animals in their natural habitat visit a wildlife sanctuary that does not buy, sell or breed animals. Instead they take in injured wildlife, unwanted exotic pets or surplus animals from zoos.

♦ Wildlife encounters at zoos might be an unforgettable experience for children or adults but they are stressful and can be harmful to the animals.

♦ Zoo animals can escape. Not only is this dangerous for people and native wildlife, but the animals are often killed rather than tranquillised.

♦ Zoo visitors often don't act responsibly and put the animals' lives in danger due to their stupidity or lack of care. When a toddler fell into an enclosure at Cincinnati Zoo in 2016 there was a worldwide outcry that Harambe, the gorilla whose enclosure the toddler fell into, was shot and killed.

The difference between zoos, safari parks and wildlife sanctuaries

What is a Zoo?

'an area in which animals, especially wild animals, are kept so that people can go and look at them or study them'

What is a Safari Park?

'a large park where wild animals are kept and can move freely, and can be watched by visitors driving through in their cars'

What is a Wildlife Sanctuary?

'a place where birds or animals can live and be protected, especially from being hunted or dangerous conditions'

Definitions from the *Cambridge English Dictionary*

So, should zoos still exist?

I don't think that zoos should need to exist. But for those that do actually rehabilitate wildlife and protect endangered species I think there is an argument for them in today's world. However, it would be far better if they were to become wildlife sanctuaries and they stopped buying and selling animals. What we should be doing is protecting the habitats of wild animals and ensuring their survival in the wild. But until people around the world care more about life than money I'm afraid there's little chance of certain species surviving without a helping hand from zoos.

That's not to say that I think all existing zoos should still exist or that most of them are adequate. I believe there are many zoos that should be shut down immediately and the majority of 'good zoos' still need to make massive improvements to their facilities. In my opinion, a zoo's major function should not be to make money for its owner. The profits from ticket prices should go toward increasing animal welfare standards, increasing enclosure sizes and protecting the natural habitats of wild animals.

I hope that in the not too distant future we see the end of zoos. Sadly I don't feel like it'll happen in my lifetime… We have too many people in power around the world for whom animal welfare and conservation is of little concern.

31 March 2020

The above information is reprinted with kind permission from Green Eco Friend.
© 2020 Green Eco Friend

www.greenecofriend.co.uk

Europe's 'Tiger Kings': new report highlights scale of captive tigers in the EU

By Matthew Holroyd

The number of captive tigers in Europe and the US is more than double the number left in the wild, according to a new report.

There are at least 1,600 captive tigers in Europe, compared to just 3,900 wild globally, says the global animal welfare organisation, FOUR PAWS.

FOUR PAWS states that tigers and cubs are being used as photo props and for selfies at facilities in countries including France, Germany, Spain and Malta.

'We know of one place where it is €50 for 10 minutes with a big cat cub,' said Kieran Harkin, Head of Wildlife Animals in Trade at FOUR PAWS International.

It is estimated that many tigers eventually 'lose their commercial value' and their body parts are sold for use in 'traditional medicine' in Asian markets like China and Vietnam.

Previous data from 2018 had officially documented only 698 captive tigers in Europe, according to the Convention on the International Trade in Endangered Species of Wild Fauna and Flora (CITES).

The new report comes just one month after a controversial Netflix true crime documentary 'Tiger King' exposed the breeding and trade of tigers in the United States.

FOUR PAWS told Euronews their concern that the demand for breeding cubs could result in a 'never-ending cycle'.

Horror stories of tigers being driven 'in the back of cars'

The private ownership of exotic pets, and the use of tigers in circuses, is still legal in a number of EU countries, but FOUR PAWS says the trade is 'poorly regulated and monitored' and many animals are suffering abuse in terrible conditions.

'It's quite easy for anyone to source and purchase a tiger in countries where private keeping is still legal,' Kieran Harkin told Euronews.

'You only need to show enclosures and some authorities are not qualified enough to check if these enclosures are adequate enough for a tiger's welfare.'

While owners usually have to apply for import and export permits, Kieran Harkin says the European Union offers an exemption to this across borders.

'There are very few checks and we have heard all sorts of horror stories of people driving tigers and other big cat species in the back of cars.'

Most European countries also require prospective owners to have a licence for keeping a dangerous animal, but Harkin says the application and issuing of these licences is 'also quite an easy process.'

FOUR PAWS also told Euronews that the sale of tigers for commercial gain can be a 'highly lucrative industry'.

A live tiger captive-bred in Europe can reportedly be worth up to €22,000, while a kilo of tiger bones could be valued at €1,700.

Which European countries have the most captive tigers?

CITES prohibits the commercial trade of wild tigers, and aims to ensure that any legal trade of tigers and parts has no impact on the survival of the species. But captive tigers are listed under a separate CITES Appendix, which does allow for their legal trade.

The Czech Republic and Germany have reported the highest figures of captive tigers in Europe, with 180 and 164 respectively.

Meanwhile, the United Kingdom, where the private keeping of captive tigers is legal, is third in the continent with 123 recorded animals.

Slovakia also reported 119 captive tigers, despite CITES recording just 3 in the EU country in 2018.

Just 17 of the 36 European countries contacted by FOUR PAWS, including only 12 EU member states, responded with figures.

NGOs estimate that Italy, one of those countries which did not respond, has 400 tigers kept in zoos, private homes and circuses.

FOUR PAWS says that many captive animals cannot be rehabilitated into the wild, while their illegal trade also fuels the demand for worldwide poaching of wild tigers.

'There will always be a higher onus on a wild tiger than a captive tiger, so by stimulating a greater demand for captive tigers, you're actually placing more threat on wild populations,' said Harkin.

'More efforts are needed,' admits the EU as further measures considered

FOUR PAWS has urgently called on the European Union to 'suspend the export and re-export of live tigers and tiger parts', except to legitimate sanctuaries.

The animal welfare organisation has further recommended that the EU introduces a comprehensive ban on commercial tiger trade to combat animal abuse.

'We need the EU to turn off the tap and stop this influx of tigers, and stop this breeding and distribution of tigers for different reasons, for circuses, for private keeping, and for petting across Europe,' Harkin told Euronews.

'If we stop the commercial trade, and the only tigers that we see or are being bred across Europe have a legitimate conservation process, then that's the ideal situation.'

'We do not need to be petting tigers, breeding hybrids and all this other entertainment.'

FOUR PAWS has previously launched projects focusing on the suffering of animals which are kept in inappropriate conditions, as well as in disaster and conflict zones.

The European Commission adopted an Action Plan against Wildlife Trafficking in February 2016 to improve efforts against wildlife crime in the EU.

But despite encouraging signs, the Commission has said that 'more efforts are needed' to combat the illegal trade of exotic animals.

'Wildlife trafficking continues to pose a serious threat to biodiversity, the rule of law and sustainable development, said Karmenu Vella, European Commissioner for the Environment, Maritime Affairs and Fisheries, in 2018.

'We need to further intensify our efforts to reach the objectives of the Action Plan by 2020, and meet the target of the UN 2030 Agenda for Sustainable Development.'

'The European Union have been very good, working in other areas of the world when it comes to illegal wildlife trade,' said Harkin, 'but it needs to look internally at its own jurisdictions'.

'We need a greater political appetite to do more and greater enforcement in Europe.'

Progress on the European Commission action plan is due to be assessed later this year. In a further statement to Euronews, a Commission source agreed that tigers need to be strictly protected.

'The Commission has therefore closely followed the recent cases of illegal trade in tigers in several EU Member States, and facilitated the exchange of relevant information among enforcement authorities through its expert group on wildlife trade enforcement.'

The EU say that, while there is no central register of tigers kept in the EU, authorities with Member States have the responsibility and capability to control the keeping and breeding of tigers.

'The Commission has intensified its cooperation with the relevant enforcement authorities of the Member States and has asked them to pay special attention to these issues.'

'[We] will continue to monitor the situation, together with the CITES authorities of EU Member States, and will consider whether further measures at EU level are needed.'

FOUR PAWS says they are also reaching out to members of the public to not take part in private interactions with big cats and recognise that 'these are not acceptable places in the modern world'.

'If it is your dream to interact with wildlife, do it in the wild - it does not compare with seeing a big cat in a sad state in a cage,' Kieran Harkin told Euronews.

'There are legitimate sanctuaries and places to go and see the animals, and it is not in your own home.'

22 April 2020

The above information is reprinted with kind permission from euronews.
© euronews 2020

www.euronews.com

Pets: is it ethical to keep them?

An article from *The Conversation*.

THE CONVERSATION

By Corey Lee Wrenn, Lecturer of Sociology, University of Kent

According to the UK veterinary charity The People's Dispensary for Sick Animals (PDSA), half of Britons own a pet. Many of these owners view the 11.1m cats, 8.9m dogs, and 1m rabbits sharing their homes as family members. But although we love them, care for them, celebrate their birthdays and mourn them when they pass, is it ethical to keep pets in the first place? Some animal rights activists and ethicists, myself included, would argue that it is not.

The institution of pet-keeping is fundamentally unjust as it involves the manipulation of animals' bodies, behaviours and emotional lives. For centuries, companion animals' bodies (particularly dogs, horses and rabbits) have been shaped to suit human fashions and fancies. And this often causes these animals considerable physical harm.

Particular breeds, for instance, are highly susceptible to painful and frequently fatal genetic defects. Highly prized physical features – such as small and large stature or pushed-in noses – can cause discomfort and difficulty in breathing, birthing and other normal functions.

Even those animals who are not purpose-bred often face bodily manipulations which impede their comfort and safety. This can include confining clothing, painful leashes that pull at the throat, docked tails and ears, and declawing, which involves the severing of the first digit of each toe in cats. Pets are also often constrained in their daily movements, sometimes crated or caged, and regularly kept indoors – always at the whim of their human owners.

Pets also symbolically reinforce the notion that vulnerable groups can be owned and fully controlled for the pleasure and convenience of more privileged and powerful groups. And this has implications for vulnerable human groups. For instance, sexism is partially maintained by treating women linguistically as pets – 'kitten', 'bunny' – and physically by confining them to the home to please and serve the family patriarch.

Social workers further recognise the powerful link between pet abuse and the abuse of children and women in domestic settings. The idea that it is acceptable to manipulate the bodies and minds of a vulnerable group to suit the interests of more privileged groups is consistent with the cultural logic of oppression.

Cannot consent

Through this forced dependency and domestication, the lives of companion animals are almost completely controlled by humans. They can be terminated at any time for the most trivial of reasons – including behavioural 'problems', for belonging to a stereotyped breed, or the owner's inability (or unwillingness) to pay for veterinary treatment.

In the mid 20th century, sociologist Erving Goffman introduced the concept of a 'total institution'. This sees inhabitants cut off from wider society under a single authority in an enclosed social space. Natural barriers between social spheres are artificially eliminated and an intense socialisation process takes place to ensure that inmates conform.

Sociologists typically study prisons, asylums and other physical spaces as examples. But I believe pet-keeping constitutes a sort of dispersed 'total institution'. This is because nonhuman animals are unnaturally forced under human authority, restrained and re-socialised. True consent is not possible under such conditions. Animals are groomed to participate and those who are unable to follow the rules of human social life are likely to be punished – sometimes fatally.

This is not in any way to suggest that dogs, cats and other species cannot express love and happiness as 'pets'. But it is important to recognise that their complacency within the institution of pet-keeping is entirely manufactured (sometimes quite cruelly) by humans through behaviour 'corrections' and the manipulative process of domestication itself.

A world without pets?

Some companion animal advocates, such as Nathan Winograd, the director of the US based No Kill Advocacy Center, argue that to stop keeping pets altogether would be a violation of nonhuman animals' right to exist. Winograd believes the widespread killing of healthy companion animals can be curbed through a restructuring of the sheltering industry. He rejects the need to end pet-keeping given the abundance of humanity's capacity for compassion and adoption.

Winograd's pro-pet position reflects the No Kill movement's strong disapproval of some animal rights organisations, which frequently support 'euthanasia' policies to curb pet populations. But if a No Kill society were to be achieved, many of the ethical violations – bodily manipulation, non-consensual confinement, enforced dependency, and vulnerability to human abuse – would remain. Even if, as Winograd supposes, an increase in legal protections could be obtained to improve domestic animals' standards of living.

Ultimately, companion animals, by their very position in the social order, are not and cannot be equals. The institution of pet-keeping maintains a social hierarchy which privileges humans and positions all others as objects of lower importance – whose right to existence depends wholly on their potential to benefit humans. That said, the population of dogs, cats, rabbits and other domesticated 'pet' animals currently rivals that of humans such that they are likely to remain a consistent feature of human social life.

And while it may not be ethical to pursue the future breeding of nonhuman animals for comfort, humans do have a duty to serve, protect and care for them. Recognising the inherent inequality in human and nonhuman relations will be vital in making the best of an imperfect situation.

25 April 2019

The above information is reprinted with kind permission from The Conversation.
© 2010-2020, The Conversation Trust (UK) Limited

www.theconversation.com

Key Facts

- The UK has dropped a grade in the second revised edition of the Animal Protection Index (API). Page 6

- The Animal Welfare Act 2006 (England and Wales) and Animal Health and Welfare (Scotland) 2006 make a pet owner legally responsible for making sure any domesticated animal under their care has their welfare needs met. Page 8

- Globally each year we farm 70 billion farm animals for meat, milk or eggs. Page 9

- In the UK we have 51 million pets. Page 10

- In London cats are the most popular pet. Page 10

- 49% of UK pet owners have stated that they believe their pet is a family member . Page 11

- In the UK we have almost 20 million cats and dogs as pets. Page 12

- After animal testing, any new drug is tested on 3-5,000 human volunteers. Page 16

- UK law requires that all medicines should be tested in at least two different species of live animals before their use in humans. Page 17

- In 2017, 9.39 million mice, rats, fish, dogs, and other animals were used for the first time in cruel experiments and other scientific procedures. Page 19

- In 2017 in the UK alone, 1.81 million animals either were bred for laboratory use but didn't fit the 'right' criteria at the 'right' time or were killed so that their body parts could be used in experiments. Page 19

- Worldwide, an estimated 500,000 animals are still suffering for cleaning products – including some in Britain. Page 20

- In 2017, there were 450 animal experiments for household product ingredients in the UK. Page 20

- 40 countries including India, New Zealand, South Korea, Switzerland, and Australia, have banned the sale of cosmetics containing ingredients tested on animals. Page 20

- In 2019, there were 3.40 million procedures completed on living animals in Great Britain. This is a decrease of 3% from last year, and the lowest number of procedures since 2007. Page 23

- In 2019, 984,000 experimental procedures were carried out for basic research purposes. Page 24

- Almost all (over 99%) of the procedures for the creation and breeding of GA animals involved mice (87%), fish (12%), or rats (0.5%). Page 24

- Thirty-one countries worldwide and 18 EU countries have banned the use of wild animals in circuses. Page 26

- 65 per cent of Europeans condemn the use of wild animals in circuses. Page 26

- The RSPCA revealed that it has looked into almost 28,168 complaints about the illegal puppy trade in the last 10 years. Page 28

- The top five hunted species are the Nile crocodile, American black bear, African elephant, hippopotamus and zebra. Page 29

- 93% of Brits don't wear real animal fur. Page 30

- 72% support a complete ban on the sale of fur in the UK. Page 30

- Since the ban came into effect in 2003, almost £800 million of fur has been imported into the UK from fur farms in France, Italy, Poland, China and other countries. Page 30

- In 2018 almost £75 million of animal fur was imported into the UK. Page 30

- Out of WAZA's 1,200 venues, 75 per cent of them had at least one practice that researchers considered seriously detrimental to the animal's wellbeing. Page 33

- There are at least 1,600 captive tigers in Europe, compared to just 3,900 wild globally. Page 36

- A live tiger captive-bred in Europe can reportedly be worth up to €22,000, while a kilo of tiger bones could be valued at €1,700. Page 36

- The Czech Republic and Germany have reported the highest figures of captive tigers in Europe, with 180 and 164 respectively. Page 36

Animal research

The process of using animals in scientific research. Also called 'animal experimentation' or 'animal testing'. Animal research for the purposes of testing cosmetic products is largely banned in the European Union. However, the use of animals in research and testing for medical purposes is still considered essential by the majority of the scientific community.

Animal rights

This term usually refers to the view that animals should be respected and treated in the same way as human beings. Animal rights campaigners reject the treatment of animals as property and campaign for their recognition as legal beings.

Animal rights extremists

Animal rights extremists object to the exploitation of animals by human beings, and in recent years their particular focus has been the use of animals in medical tests by pharmaceutical companies. Extremists have been known to use tactics including death threats, planting bombs and destroying property against pharmaceutical workers and their families.

Animal Welfare Act 2006/2007

Passed in 2006, this animal welfare legislation came into force in 2007. Whilst it largely repealed and replaced the 1911 Protection of Animals Act, the law also made it an offence to fail to ensure the welfare of an animal, and to dock the whole, or any part, of a dog's tail. Anyone found guilty of committing offences could be banned from owning animals, fined up to £20,000 and/or given a prison sentence.

Cosmetics and animal testing

Some companies test their products on animals to ensure that their products are safe for use by humans (not just in cosmetics, but in other toiletries, detergents, etc. as well). Animal rights activists oppose this testing because of the potential harm done to the animal subjects. The testing of cosmetics and their ingredients on animals is banned in the European Union, India, Israel and Norway. Cruelty-free products carry the 'leaping bunny' logo to show that they have not been tested on animals. This includes brands such as LUSH and The Body Shop.

Factory farming

A method of farming where a large number of animals are confined within small spaces such as cages, crates and overcrowded sheds. The animals are specifically bred for the purpose of being 'factory farmed' and this means that there are breeds which are selected because they are fast growing or high producing.

Fake fur (Faux fur)

First introduced in 1929, fake fur mimics the appearance and feel of fur. Often made of plastic, fake fur can be detrimental to the environment.

Hunting

Hunting is the killing or animals for food or sport. Includes trophy hunting, where people kill animals and keep and display their body parts.

Intensive farming

Intensive farming involves high levels of input (labour and cost) in order to maximise output of a product. In livestock farming, this can mean large numbers of animals cramped into a very limited space. This is sometimes called factory farming, and has been criticised for its disregard for the welfare of animals.

Non-human animals (also Nonhuman animals)

Any animal that is not a human being.

Personhood

The state of being a person, which in turn entitles them to have basic legal (and human) rights. Reactions to treating nonhuman animals as persons vary widely. Some people think it is ridiculous to even entertain the idea as they feel that persons have to be human. For others, they believe the criteria of personhood includes being rational, self-aware, autonomous, having culture and being able to communicate. Chimpanzees and dolphins, for example, display these traits and by arguing that they be given the status of persons, they will in turn be granted basic rights (e.g. chimpanzees would no longer be kept for research and could be moved to a sanctuary).

Puppy farm

Sometimes referred to as a puppy mill, this is a place where large-scale breeding of puppies takes place.; a breeder who breeds puppies on a high volume and intensive basis. Usually with little or no regard for the health and welfare of the puppies or the parents, the main intent is to make money.

RSPCA

Originally known as the Society for the Prevention of Cruelty to Animals (SPCA), founded in 1824, the SPCA later became the Royal Society for the Prevention of Cruelty to Animals after receiving royal patronage by Queen Victoria. The charity works to rescue and rehabilitate thousands of animals each year, offer advice on caring for all animals and campaign for their protection.

Vivisection

The act or practice of cutting into or performing surgery on living animals for the purpose of scientific research

Wild Animals in Circuses Bill

This bill aims to ban the use of wild animals in circuses, such as lions, tigers, camels, etc. The argument is, aside from the concern about animal welfare, that it has no educational, conversational or research benefit – it's all just for entertainment. On the other hand, Mr Rosindell, MP for Romford, has argued that the circus is a 'Great British institution…[that] deserves to be defended against the propaganda and exaggerations'. Whilst the majority of the public supports a ban, as do most MPs, the bill has been blocked by the government for now and will need to be reintroduced under the next government.

Activities

Brainstorming

♦ In small groups, discuss what you know about animal rights and welfare.

  · What is animal welfare?

  · What are animal rights?

  · Are humans and animals equal?

  · What is the Animal Welfare Act 2006?

  · If a product is 'cruelty-free', what does this mean? How do you know if a product is 'cruelty-free'?

Research

♦ Research animal rights organisations in your local area. Are they local or national charities? How do they raise awareness for their cause?

♦ Create a questionnaire to find out how many and what type of pets your friends and family may have.

♦ Create a questionnaire to find out your friends' and family's opinions on animal testing. Do any of them support it? Are some animals seen as less important than others when it comes to testing?

♦ Do some research on which animals are used for sport or entertainment; you could look at circuses, zoos or hunting as an example.

♦ Do some research into which companies are cruelty free. How can you tell?

♦ Choose a fast food restaurant and have a look at their animal welfare standards.

Design

♦ Design a PowerPoint presentation exploring the issues surrounding the use of animals and animal bi-products for food, medicine, entertainment, cosmetics and clothing. You should consider the benefits and disadvantages, as well as your own opinion.

♦ Design a poster that summarises UK animal rights issues.

♦ Choose one of the articles from this topic and create an illustration that highlights the key themes of the piece.

♦ Design a poster to persuade people to look for cruelty free products. Show the different symbols used.

♦ Design a leaflet with the Pros and Cons for animal experimentation.

Oral

♦ As a class, discuss whether animals should have the same rights as humans or not.

♦ Organise a class debate on the pros and cons of zoos. Use the article 'Should zoos still exist?' as well as your own further research as inspiration. One half of your class will represent zoo supporters and the other will represent the campaigners who want zoos to be abolished.

♦ Organise a class debate on the pros and cons of wearing fur. One half of the class will oppose, the other will be in favour.

♦ In small groups, discuss whether animals should be used for entertainment or not.

♦ In pairs, discuss the five welfare needs and list how they can be met.

Reading/writing

♦ Write a persuasive letter to a company that tests its products on animals. Include the reasons why you think this is/is not a good idea.

♦ Imagine you are writing an article about intensive farming. How can you persuade your reader to buy free range or high welfare products?

♦ Imagine that a circus is coming to town and that they use animals in their show. Write a letter to your local newspaper saying why you think it should not go ahead.

♦ Think of a time where you might have seen an animal suffering. Write a diary entry on how that made you feel and what you might do about it.

♦ Read *Eva* by Peter Dickinson; write a book review.

♦ Watch a documentary such as *Prince William: A Planet for Us All* or *A Life on Our Planet*. Write how these made you feel. Will you change your opinion on animal rights?

First published by Independence Educational Publishers

The Studio, High Green

Great Shelford

Cambridge CB22 5EG

England

© Independence 2020

Copyright

This book is sold subject to the condition that it shall not,
by way of trade or otherwise, be lent, resold, hired out or otherwise
circulated in any form of binding or cover other than that in which it
is published without the publisher's prior consent.

Photocopy licence

The material in this book is protected by copyright. However, the
purchaser is free to make multiple copies of particular articles for instructional
purposes for immediate use within the purchasing institution.
Making copies of the entire book is not permitted.

ISBN-13: 978 1 86168 835 4

Printed in Great Britain

Zenith Print Group

Contents

Introduction

Ageing is Volume 378 in the **issues** series. The aim of the series is to offer current, diverse information about important issues in our world, from a UK perspective.

ABOUT Ageing

No matter how hard we try to prevent it, all of us are getting older. In less than 20 years one in four people in the UK will be over 65. But what issues do people come across as they age? Older people often experience things such as discrimination or health problems that can make life much harder for them. This book explores living longer and how we can all live a healthy, happy long life.

OUR SOURCES

Titles in the **issues** series are designed to function as educational resource books, providing a balanced overview of a specific subject.

The information in our books is comprised of facts, articles and opinions from many different sources, including:

♦ Newspaper reports and opinion pieces

♦ Website factsheets

♦ Magazine and journal articles

♦ Statistics and surveys

♦ Government reports

♦ Literature from special interest groups.

A NOTE ON CRITICAL EVALUATION

Because the information reprinted here is from a number of different sources, readers should bear in mind the origin of the text and whether the source is likely to have a particular bias when presenting information (or when conducting their research). It is hoped that, as you read about the many aspects of the issues explored in this book, you will critically evaluate the information presented.

It is important that you decide whether you are being presented with facts or opinions. Does the writer give a biased or unbiased report? If an opinion is being expressed, do you agree with the writer? Is there potential bias to the 'facts' or statistics behind an article?

ASSIGNMENTS

In the back of this book, you will find a selection of assignments designed to help you engage with the articles you have been reading and to explore your own opinions. Some tasks will take longer than others and there is a mixture of design, writing and research-based activities that you can complete alone or in a group.

FURTHER RESEARCH

At the end of each article we have listed its source and a website that you can visit if you would like to conduct your own research. Please remember to critically evaluate any sources that you consult and consider whether the information you are viewing is accurate and unbiased.

Useful Websites

www.agewatch.net

www.ageing-better.org.uk

www.bestadvice.co.uk

www.blogs.lse.ac.uk

www.brookings.edu

www.fullfact.org

www.homecare.co.uk

www.independentage.org

www.independent.co.uk

www.inews.co.uk

www.lovemoney.com

www.nhs.uk

www.ons.gov.uk

www.platinumskies.co.uk

www.theconversation.com

www.theguardian.com

www.telegraph.co.uk

www.worldatlas.com

www.yorkpress.co.uk

Living longer: is age 70 the new age 65?

Measuring ageing in terms of remaining life expectancy, instead of years lived, may provide a better indicator of the health of our ageing population.

When does older age begin?

In the UK, 65 years of age has traditionally been taken as the marker for the start of older age, most likely because it was the official retirement age for men and the age at which they could draw their State Pension.

In terms of working patterns, age 65 years as the start of older age is out of date. There is no longer an official retirement age, State Pension age is rising, and increasing numbers of people work past the age of 65 years.

People are also living longer, healthier lives. In 2018, a man aged 65 could expect to live for another 18.6 years, while a woman could expect to live for 21 more years. So, on average, at age 65 years, women still have a quarter of their lives left to live and men just over one fifth.

An important further consideration is that age 65 years is not directly comparable over time; someone aged 65 years today has different characteristics, particularly in terms of their health and life expectancy, than someone the same age a century ago.

In a number of respects, it could be argued that the start of older age has shifted, but how might this be determined? Should we just move the threshold on a few years – is age 70 really the new age 65? Or, might there be a better way of determining the start of older age?

What is population ageing?

At a population level, ageing is measured by an increase in the number and proportion of those aged 65 years and over, and an increase in median age (the age at which half the population is younger and half older).

On both of these measures, the population has aged and is projected to continue to age (Figure 1). In 2018, there were 11.9 million residents in Great Britain aged 65 years and over, representing 18% of the total population. This compares with the middle of the 20th century (1950) when there were 5.3 million people of this age, accounting for 10.8% of the population.

Looking ahead to the middle of this century, there are projected to be 17.7 million people aged 65 years and over

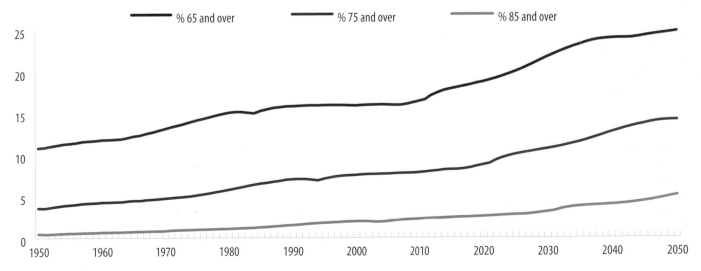

Figure 1: The percentage of older people in Great Britain has been increasing since the middle of the 20th century

Percentage of people aged 65 years and over, 75 years and over, and 85 years and over, 1950 to 2050, Great Britain

Source: Office for National Statistics

(24.8% of the population). The oldest old are the fastest-growing age group, with the numbers of those aged 85 years and over projected to double from 1.6 million in 2018 to 3.6 million by 2050 (5% of the population).

The balance of older and younger people in the population has also tipped more towards older people, reflected in a rising median age up from 34 years in 1950 to 40 years in 2018. By the middle of this century it is projected that median age will reach 43 years.

Why does population ageing matter?

Measuring population ageing is important because it has multiple economic, public service and societal impacts. It brings challenges but also opportunities.

From an economic and societal point of view, longer lives mean people can continue to contribute for longer – through longer working lives, volunteering, and possibly providing care for family members, for example, grandchildren. For individuals it might mean the opportunity to spend more time with family and friends and to pursue personal interests with more time for leisure activities.

When considering the challenges, more older people means increased demand for health and adult social services, and increased public spending on State Pensions. The key to shifting the balance from challenge towards opportunity, both at a societal level and at an individual level, is for older people to be able to live healthy lives for as long as possible.

Is there a better measure of population ageing?

Sergei Scherbov and Warren Sanderson have suggested that instead of taking a fixed chronological age as the start of older age, a better alternative would be to set the threshold at a fixed remaining life expectancy (RLE) of 15 years.

The age at which a person has an RLE of 15 years changes over time in line with changes in life expectancy and will also be different for men and women because of differences in their life expectancies.

In 2017, in Great Britain a man with RLE of 15 years was aged 70 and a woman was aged 72. In terms of RLE this is equivalent to a man aged 57 and a woman aged 60 in 1911. It is projected that by 2066, the equivalent ages will be 75 years for a man and 77 years for a woman.

Unlike chronological age, age at RLE15 is a measure that changes over time in line with improvements in life

expectancies. Instead of looking back over years lived (chronological age), this measure looks forward and marks the start of older age in terms of an average number of years left to live, that is, a prospective measure of ageing.

Is age 70 the new age 65?

Men aged 70 years in 2017 had a remaining life expectancy (RLE) of 15 years and women aged 70 years an RLE of 17 years. In terms of prospective ages (RLE) a man aged 70 years today is equivalent to a man aged 65 years in 1997 and a woman aged 70 years is equivalent to a woman aged 65

Age at which remaining life expectancy is 15 for men, and 17 for women, selected years, Great Britain

	Men	Women
1911	57.8	57.4
1951	59.0	60.6
1981	62.0	65.0
1997	65.0	66.8
2017	70.0	70.0
2037	72.9	72.3
2057	75.0	74.1

Source: Office for National Statistics
Notes: Data for years prior to 1981 are for England and Wales only.

years in 1981. But is 70 really the new 65? Did a man aged 65 years in 1997 have the same characteristics as a man aged 70 years today? And does a woman aged 70 years today have the same characteristics as a woman aged 65 years in 1981?

Arguably, the most important characteristics to consider, both from an individual and a population perspective, is level of health. This is because health has such a great impact on the choices an individual can make (for example, to work longer and participate in the activities they enjoy) and at a societal level, it drives the demand for health and social care services and the potential for people to have longer working lives.

Age at which there is 15 years of remaining life expectancy

	1911	2017	2066
Men	57	70	75
Women	60	72	77

Source: Office for National Statistics

Women aged 70 years in 2017 have similar levels of limiting longstanding illness as women aged 64 years in 1981

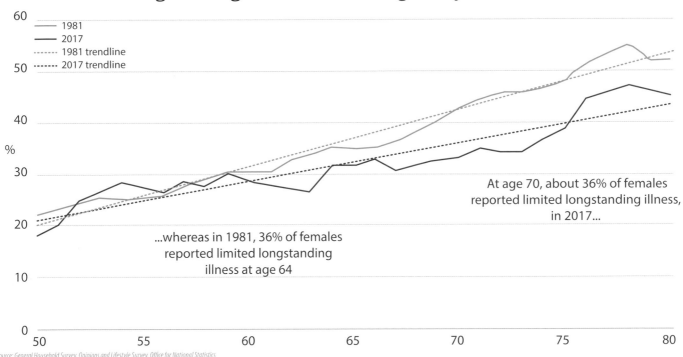

- 1981
- 2017
- 1981 trendline
- 2017 trendline

At age 70, about 36% of females reported limited longstanding illness, in 2017...

...whereas in 1981, 36% of females reported limited longstanding illness at age 64

Source: General Household Survey, Opinions and Lifestyle Survey, Office for National Statistics

Previous research has suggested that some aspects of health are more closely related to years of life remaining than years lived (chronological age). Does this mean that measures based on prospective age are a fairer measure of population ageing, in terms of health, than those based on chronological age? If this is the case, we would expect to see health by chronological age improving over time with health by prospective ages (RLEs) showing less change.

Likewise, we would expect 70-year-old men today to have around the same level of health as 65-year-old men in 1997 and women aged 70 years today to have similar health to 65-year-old women in 1981.

Is age 70 the new age 65 in terms of health?

Returning to the question we posed earlier, is 70 the new 65? In terms of remaining life expectancies, a man aged 70 years in 2017 has the same prospective age as a man aged 65 years in 1997 and a woman aged 70 years in 2017 has the same prospective age as a woman aged 65 years in 1981. But how does their health status compare?

Levels of poor general health for women aged 70 years in 2017 were around the same as for those aged 60 years in 1981, while levels of limiting long-standing illness were similar for women aged around 64 years

19 November 2019

The above information is reprinted with kind permission from the Office for National Statistics.
© Crown copyright 2020
This information is licensed under the Open Government Licence v3.0
To view this licence, visit http://www.nationalarchives.gov.uk/doc/open-government-licence/ OGL

www.ons.gov.uk

How long can humans live?

An article from *The Conversation*.

By Anthony Medford, Postdoctoral associate researcher, University of Southern Denmark, James W Vaupel, Professor of Demography and Epidemiology, University of Southern Denmark and Kaare Christensen, Director of the Danish Aging Research Center and the Danish Twin Register, University of Southern Denmark

THE CONVERSATION

Humans are living longer around the world. While there have been obvious ups and downs, life expectancy at birth overall has been steadily increasing for many years. It has more than doubled in the last two centuries.

This increase was previously driven by reductions in infant mortality. But since around the 1950s, the main driver has been reductions in mortality at older ages. In Sweden, for example, where national population data have been collected since the mid-16th century and are of a very high quality, the maximum lifespan has been increasing for almost 150 years. Increasing lifespans have been observed in many other countries, including in Western Europe, North America and Japan.

This has contributed to a rapid increase in the number of very old people – those living up to 100, 110 or even more. The first verified supercentenarian (aged 110 and above) was Geert Adrians-Boomgaard, who died in 1899 aged 110 years, four months. His record has been broken by others since. The first verified female supercentenarian, Margaret Ann Neve, died in 1903 aged 110 years, ten months and held the record for almost 23 years. Delina Filkins passed away in 1928 aged 113 years, seven months. She kept the record for just over 52 years.

The current record holder is the French woman Jeanne Calment, who died on August 4, 1997, aged 122 years, five months. Despite the near exponential increase in the number of supercentenarians since the early 1970s, her record holds firm – but she's unlikely to hold it for much longer.

Surviving past 100

Although these upward lifespan trends are widespread, they are not a given. Recent improvements in Danish mortality after a period of stagnation has led to the suspicion that centenarian lifespans could be increasing there. This is rather different from what has been recently observed in Sweden, where there has been some slow down at the highest ages.

We studied 16,931 centenarians (10,955 Swedes and 5,976 Danes) born between 1870 and 1904 in Denmark and Sweden, neighbouring countries with close cultural and historical ties, to see if our suspicions may be correct. Although Sweden generally has lower mortality rates than Denmark at most ages, no evidence of an increase in Sweden was found in recent years. In Denmark, however, the very oldest were observed to die at higher and higher ages, and the age at which only 6% of centenarians survive rose consistently over the period.

Denmark and Sweden are similar in many ways, yet these lifespan trends are very different. The disparity could be due to several causes, which are not easy to fully disentangle. But we have a few ideas.

Health systems

First, there are different levels of health among the two elderly populations. Recent studies have shown improvements in health as measured by Activities of Daily Living (ADL) – the basic tasks necessary for leading an independent life, such as bathing or getting dressed – in cohorts of female centenarians in Denmark. In Sweden, by contrast, such trends for the elderly have been less optimistic. One study found that there was no improvement in ADL, with deterioration in mobility, cognition and performance tests.

The difference in the two healthcare systems, especially in recent times, could therefore also go some way towards explaining the difference. Spending on public services was reduced in Sweden in the early 1990s, due to a series of economic crises. Healthcare for the elderly was affected. For instance, with inpatient elder care, there was a shift away from hospitals to nursing homes and a reduction in the number of nursing home beds. The cost cuts left some older people at risk, particularly those in the lowest socioeconomic groups.

In addition, the two countries have since followed slightly different paths to elderly care: Sweden tends to target the frailest whereas Denmark takes a slightly broader approach. Some studies suggest that Sweden's approach has resulted in some who require care not receiving it, with the least well-off segments of the elderly population relying more heavily on family care, which can be of lower quality.

People who reach advanced ages are a select group and are obviously very durable. Perhaps because of their inherent resilience and particular physiology, they are best able to benefit from the improvements in living conditions and technology.

Our comparative study suggests some interesting things for other nations, particularly where there are developing and emerging economies. These findings demonstrate that it may be possible to lengthen lifespans further if improvements in health at the highest ages can be realised and if high quality elderly care is widely available. Indeed, if this is so, then the human longevity revolution is set to continue for some time still.

29 May 2019

The above information is reprinted with kind permission from The Conversation.
© 2010-2020, The Conversation Trust (UK) Limited

www.theconversation.com

Living into the 22nd century

By Wolfgang Fengler

At the beginning of each new year, UNICEF organizes a global campaign to celebrate the birth of the year's first babies. This time, we cheered the arrival of 2020 and of a little over 392,000 new babies. The average life expectancy of a girl born today is 79.6 years—for a boy it is 76.2 years—which means that she and her peers will live to shape the rest of this century. And one thing is clear: These newborns of the decade will live in a fundamentally different world than the one their parents knew.

In most parts of the world, these newborns will grow up to be healthier, wealthier, and better educated than their parents. They will also live longer. Over the last two decades, life expectancy has already increased from 71 to 78 years, with the greatest gains made in emerging economies. The well-informed reader may wonder why these estimates are substantially higher than the projections often quoted from official sources such as national statistical agencies or the U.N.'s population division. The answer lies in the projection method. The traditional approach is period life expectancy estimates, which calculates the average age of people dying today. This stands in contrast to cohort expectancy estimates, which projects improvements in mortality throughout a person's lifetime. The latter provides a more realistic estimate of life expectancy and results on average in almost 10 years more compared to period life expectancy estimates. This blog builds on the cohort life expectancy projections in population.io which were developed by the World Data Lab, together with the International Institute of Applied Systems Analysis (IIASA).

Almost two-thirds of today's newborns will live to see the next century.

As we enter the third decade of the 21st century, the younger among us can realistically set their sights on 2100. Even though the average global life expectancy is still below 80 years, almost two-thirds of today's newborns will live to see the next century. Once they survive the first years of their lives, they will have a significant chance to live through adulthood and into their 80s.

However, there are still wide differences across countries. A typical girl born in Singapore today can expect to live more than 97 years (until February 2117), while a boy born in Sierra Leone can only expect to live almost 40 years less (to just 58.5 years). The top three countries in terms of life expectancy are all in Asia—Singapore, Japan, South Korea—followed by European countries and Chile. The bottom 10 countries are all in sub-Saharan Africa, even though life expectancy has been rising there as well.

In Europe and North America, as well as many parts of Asia, some 80 percent of new babies will live into the next century—almost nine out of 10 girls born in Europe! If we include all of the children born in previous years who also have a chance, there are more than 900 million people alive today, who can expect to live into the next century!

The dramatic progress embedded in these statistics is obvious to all of us, especially boomers who hail from the 20th century. And yet there is still significant scope to further increase the collective chance of humans to live long and healthy lives. To realize it, we need to better understand the causes of mortality: We need to know when people die, in which country, from which cause.

Some 50 years ago, most people died from diarrhea, malaria, tuberculosis, or simple respiratory diseases. One of the big successes of development since 1970 has been the sharp fall in communicable diseases, including AIDS, over the last decade. While communicable diseases are still the leading cause of death for children and young adults—mostly in Africa and Asia—they now account for "only" some 30 percent of all deaths in any given year, approximately 18 million. Among them, the greatest killers are respiratory diseases (3.5 million), diarrhea (1.5 million), AIDS and malaria (each approximately 1 million). Meanwhile the number of deaths from road accidents has risen to 1.3 million.

By contrast, noncommunicable diseases represent 70 percent of total deaths, of which heart disease is now the largest with 20 million deaths in 2019 (32 percent), followed by cancer with approximately 8 million (13 percent). While the growth in noncommunicable disease is a sign of aging, i.e., successful development, there is an increasing number of people in emerging markets who die from noncommunicable diseases as working adults. The prevention of these diseases, such as diabetes and cancer, in adulthood will be crucial.

The health challenges that used to be confined to rich countries (heart disease, cancer, diabetes, and dementia) will start to play a bigger role across the globe. In fact, many emerging economies will experience a double burden of disease. Even though communicable diseases are on the decline, they remain elevated (e.g., in Kenya the No. 1 cause of death remains HIV/AIDS), while noncommunicable diseases and accidents are rising.

Disease and death will eventually and ultimately strike all of us. And yet they will do so very differently depending on our age, gender, and the part of the world we are born in. This is why a risk-based approach to public policy makes sense. In short: We need a better and more dynamic model for predicting at a granular level the risks that individuals will be exposed to most at each stage of their lives, wherever they are. Creating such a data model would be a great endeavour for the new decade.

14 January 2020

The above information is reprinted with kind permission from The Brookings Institution.
© 2020 The Brookings Institution

www.brookings.edu

Countries where people live the longest

By Jessica Dillinger

It is said that a desire for a long life is a universal component of human nature. Nonetheless, some parts of the world see this desire fulfilled far more often than others. In fact, only a handful of countries have life expectancies greater than 80 years. At the helm of countries with the longest life expectancy is Japan, followed by Switzerland and Spain, who all have average life expectancies of greater than 80 years. It may seem unfair that residents of certain countries have more realistic odds of long life than others, but there are a number of good reasons why this incongruity has come to be.

Measuring life expectancy

Life expectancy is determined by computing the average of the ages at which people die in a given country. As such, infant mortality rate is a key determinant factor. As a matter of fact, all the countries which have the highest life expectancy have very low infant mortality rates.

Access to health care

It goes without saying that early death, including infant mortality, is usually caused by health problems. That is why when we see countries with low life expectancies and high infant mortality rates, we often see an accompanying lack of accessibility to good health care and a generally underdeveloped medical infrastructure. The combination of factors that contribute to the general health standards of a country include not only the availability and quality of its healthcare facilities, but quality of food and pollution regulations as well.

The safety factor

Another factor that contributes positively to some countries' long life expectancies are their high levels of security. For instance, Iceland, Singapore, and Luxembourg all rank among the top ten most secure countries, each scoring greater than six on a scale from zero to seven. Obviously insecurity issues such as terrorism, organized crimes, and other violent criminal activities serve to lower the life expectancy of those countries where they are prevalent.

A high quality of life correlates to longer lives

It must be noted that the countries that have the highest life expectancy are generally the most developed countries as well. Factors lending to a high quality of life in such countries range from a modern economy, pollution control and well-developed infrastructure to quality education systems and high penetration rates of internet usage. A benefit of education in particular is that it generates awareness among citizens of the need to promote and maintain good health. Additionally, the residents of such countries not only understand the importance of nutritious food, but are more likely to be able to afford it as well. Countries that are less developed in relation to these aspects, such as many Asian and Sub-Saharan African countries, struggle to achieve similarly long life expectancies.

The bottom line is that it isn't by sheer chance that countries among our list have a relatively long life expectancy in relation to other countries. Instead, it is because of the many characteristics that they share in common that citizens of these countries can achieve long lives, and the further development of such characteristics can allow developing nations to raise their own life expectancies as well.

10 January 2019

The above information is reprinted with kind permission from World Atlas.
© 2020 World Atlas

www.worldatlas.com

Countries by life expectancy

Rank	Country	Life expectancy
1	Japan	84.2
2	Switzerland	83.3
3	Spain	83.1
4	Australia	82.9
5	France	82.9
6	Singapore	82.9
7	Canada	82.8
8	Italy	82.8
9	Republic of Korea	82.7
10	Norway	82.5
11	Iceland	82.4
12	Luxembourg	82.4
13	Sweden	82.4
14	Israel	82.3
15	New Zealand	82.2

Why do women live longer than men?

Women usually live longer than men. Why is this – and are modern day vices, such as smoking and drinking, reducing the longevity gap?

By Kayhan Nouri-Aria

Life expectancy in the UK is currently 79.6 years for men and 83.2 years for women. So why do women tend to live longer?

Male vs female hormones

♦ Young males - teens to early twenties - are fuelled with higher levels of the testosterone hormone and this is a contributory factor to men being more aggressive and competitive. Competitiveness among men also increased when attractive women are present. This results in young men taking more risks than women of a similar age, such as riding motor bikes without helmets or getting into fights – thereby increasing their risk of an early death.

♦ Testosterone works closely with cholesterol in the body and this can cause problems in later life for men. Research by the Endocrine Society, reported in 2015, has shown that high levels of testosterone leads the body to produce lower levels of 'good' cholesterol. However, testosterone does not have any impact on 'bad' cholesterol, blood pressure or body fat. This leaves the male body more susceptible to cardiovascular disease.

♦ A 2012 study, using historical data on castrated eunuchs in Korea, shows that they lived 14 years longer than their non-castrated socio economic male equivalents. This further suggests that testosterone (production of which is dramatically reduced by castration) is negatively linked to male longevity.

♦ Pre-menopausal women, on the other hand, are protected by the sex hormone oestrogen. This study explain that sex hormones, particularly oestrogen, possess potent antioxidant properties and play important roles in maintaining normal reproductive and non-reproductive functions. Furthermore oestrogen has ability to repair DNA in organs such as the brain. Another study demonstrated that oestrogen could help protect women from cardiovascular disease, by stopping white blood cells sticking to the insides of blood vessels, a process which can lead to dangerous blockages. 'The results could help explain why cardiovascular disease rates tend to be higher in men and why they soar in women after the menopause.'

Evolution

In most species, including humans, women are the main carers for the young. So from an evolutionary perspective, it is probably more important that women live longer, to ensure the wellbeing of their children and thus the survival of the human race.

As Professor Thomas Kirkwood has asked, 'could it be that women live longer because they are less disposable than men?'

Other biological factors

♦ Women have two X-chromosomes, while men only have one. This may act like an insurance policy.

♦ Women tend to be more iron deficient due to menstruation. High levels of iron encourages the formation of free radicals and an increased cancer risk. So this may also explain why women generally live longer than men. That's according to the Physicians Committee for Responsible Medicine.

Is the longevity gap between the sexes closing?

♦ Smoking is a particular risk for women. They now smoke at around the same rate as men. This is important because smoking increases the risk of chronic heart disease in both sexes - but the risk is believed to be 25% greater for women compared with men. That was the conclusion from a systematic review published in The Lancet in 2011.

♦ Alcohol, like tobacco, also disproportionately increases the health risk for women compared with men, as the US Centers for Disease Control and Prevention explains. This includes an increased risk of liver disease, brain damage, damage to the heart muscle and some cancers.

- Obesity levels have risen across most of the developed world. For women in the UK levels are similar to those for men (at 30% versus 27%). Unfortunately, obesity increases health risks for both men and women, including type 2 diabetes, and some cancers.

- Women may sometimes experience different heart disease symptoms than men and so not always recognise the risk. For example they may experience pressure or tightness in the chest rather than chest pain or other symptoms such as right arm pain, shortness of breath, nausea or sweating.

- Conversely, rising affluence and the need for less manual labour is being linked to longer life for men. For example few men in the UK are now involved in hazardous, physically demanding jobs like mining. In 2015 the UK Office for National Statistics (ONS) reported that professional and higher managerial men in the UK can expect to live for 82.5 years, one month longer than the 82.4 years of life expectancy for the average woman.

As some women adopt male patterns of smoking and drinking, perhaps not realising they are at greater risk then men; as obesity levels rise (with the knock on health effects); as women may not always recognize the different symptoms of heart disease; and as some men benefit from less physically demanding work and higher incomes, the overall gap between how long the two sexes live seems to be narrowing.

Conclusions

- Women appear to be biologically more predisposed to living longer than men.

- There may be an evolutionary reason for this i.e. women, as the primary carers, are designed to live longer to ensure the survival of the human race.

- However, women face even higher health risks from smoking and too much alcohol than men, so adopting male patterns of smoking and drinking may reduce their initial biological advantage – with obesity another risk factor.

- Women also need to check that they know the symptoms of heart disease - and how these may differ for them compared with men.

- Conversely, men who have higher incomes and less physically demanding jobs, now seem to be living as long as the average woman.

February 2020

The above information is reprinted with kind permission from Age Watch
© 2020 Age Watch

www.agewatch.net

Why do people live longer in Japan?

Why are Japanese people living so long? Can we learn any lessons from them?

How long do people live to in Japan?

What is the average life expectancy in Japan?

Japanese women have a life expectancy of 87.3 years – the second highest in the world after Hong Kong – while male life expectancy in Japan is the third highest internationally, well ahead of the US and UK.

In this article, we look at some of the possible reasons why Japan has an average life expectancy so much higher than most other countries.

Is it the Japanese diet?

A 2016 study in the British Medical Journal (BMJ) found that Japanese adults who followed government advice about diet had a 15% lower rate of mortality than those who didn't follow the advice. The diet itself is high in certain carbohydrates (such as rice and vegetables), fruits, fish and meat, and low in saturated fats, processed foods.

> **Average food portions in Japan are quite a bit smaller than in a country like the USA.**

However, in 2011 The Lancet suggested the dietary picture is more mixed. Some aspects of the Japanese diet (like a preference for highly refined rice and bread as staples) could be responsible for increasing rates of diabetes due to low dietary fibre intake and a high glycaemic index.

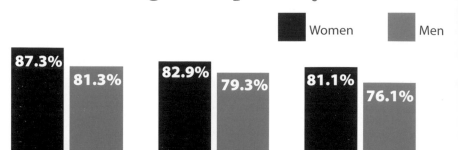

Average life expectancy

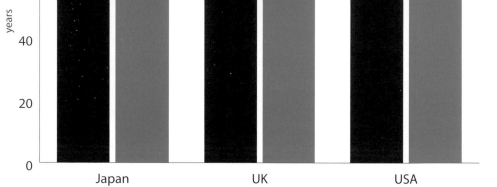

% of obese adults

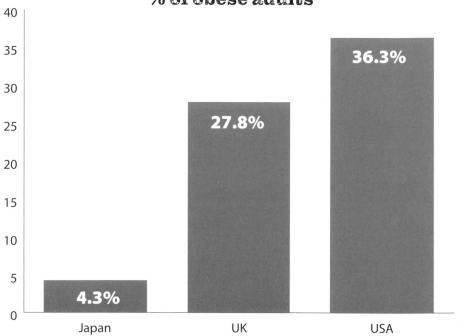

The traditional Japanese diet is also under threat as more Western food chains and Western dietary habits become popular. By 2012, the Japanese government was already concerned about the fall in the consumption of fruit and vegetables and the increase in meat consumption.

These changes have led to a rise in obesity in Japan, and as a result, an increase in the risk of hypertension (high blood pressure) as well as other adverse health outcomes, such as

breast cancers. Despite this (and assisted by lower calorie consumption), obesity rates in Japan are still very low, with fewer than 5% classed as obese compared to nearly 28% of people in the UK and 36% in the USA.

Is it Japan's healthcare system?

Since 1961 Japan has had universal healthcare, with equal and universal access to healthcare for all through a health insurance scheme which is paid for by government, employers and individuals. As such, Japan performs well when looking at the social determinants of health (the conditions in which people are born, grow, live, work and age).

In Japan, regular check-ups are the norm. Local government authorities provide mass screening for everyone at school, at work or in the community. Also, everyone has to fill in a medical questionnaire that asks specific questions about lifestyle. These annual check-ups may help people become more health conscious.

However, the financial and social underpinnings of Japan's health provisions are threatened by economic decline and widening social inequalities. Together with rising costs and an ageing population, this raises the question of how long Japan's healthcare system can remain universal.

The cost of Japan's universal healthcare is about 11% of its GDP (gross domestic product). That's more than the UK's 9.8% but well below the USA's nearly 17%. Does this mean that Japanese people are using less healthcare than their US counterparts because they are healthier, or is their healthcare system more cost effective? Either way, universal health coverage with manageable expenditure seems worth aiming for when considering the health of the nation.

What about social cohesion?

Professor Shiro Horiuchi, in Japan's Journal of Population Studies in 2011, identifies social cohesion as one factor providing a particular advantage when it comes to longevity. He acknowledges that there are growing inequalities in Japan, but he argues that:

The strong group orientation seems conducive to the psychological well-being of Japanese people with low socio-economic status. It gives them deep feelings of belongingness to organizations and communities, keeping them from feeling alienated in the society…. The feeling gives them relatively high self-esteem (in spite of their low ranks and salaries), and helps them to have positive perceptions, emotions and attitudes about their lives.

Following the effects of a quarter of a century of economic stagnation, how long this social cohesion will last is now being questioned. However, strong social cohesion seems likely to have contributed to Japanese longevity so far.

Do Japanese people exercise more?

Some studies suggest that the Japanese do not exercise more than people in other countries. For example, a 2009 study concluded that Japan was one of four countries where less than 20% of the adult population was in the high physical activity category.

However, some observers argue that everyday life in Japan involves more commuting by public transport than by car, meaning more daily exercise in Japan than, for instance, in the US. More recently, perhaps inspired by the anticipation of the now sadly cancelled 2020 Tokyo Olympics, there have been positive reports of higher levels of physical activity among children and young people.

Do Japanese people have better genes?

There is some evidence that Japanese people have good genes which aid their longevity.

Studies have suggested two genes in particular – DNA 5178 and the ND2-237Met NDgenotype – help the Japanese live longer by protecting them against some adult-onset diseases. However, this effect isn't seen across the whole population.

Other genetic factors, including personality (especially characteristics such as conscientiousness, openness and being extroverted), also seem to be important. It is suggested that they contribute to longevity through beneficial health-related behaviours, stress reduction, and adapting to the problems of growing old.

Downsides to the Japanese way of life – karoshi and karo-jisatsu

Since the 1970s, there have been discussions about karoshi: literally, death by overworking. Karoshi is brought on by heavy workloads, long working hours and stress.

Since 1987, when companies were encouraged to limit working hours, the Japanese Ministry for Labour has been publishing figures on karoshi. It was found that the biological aspects behind these work-related deaths are linked to heart disease, high blood pressure and strokes.

Not only are there deaths as a direct result of overworking, but suicide rates in Japan, especially for men, are also very high and are also linked to overworking – a death known as karo-jisatsu. These deaths are most common in managerial and administrative jobs, where stress levels are high, as well as in jobs with low social support, lack of control over work, and heavy workloads.

What health lessons can we learn from Japan?

- ♦ A healthy diet can help you live longer, wherever you live. So follow government healthy eating guidelines.

- ♦ Universal healthcare, with equal access to all (as we also have in the UK) helps extend our lives as well.

- ♦ We shouldn't underestimate the value of social cohesion - the sense of belonging to organisations and communities. We need to consider how to achieve and maintain social cohesion both as individuals and as a society.

- ♦ Avoid the factors that risk reducing longevity, such as a diet of fast food and overworking.

The above information is reprinted with kind permission from Age Watch
© 2020 Age Watch

www.agewatch.net

Real retirement ages around the world revealed

Ranked: retirement ages around the world.

The official age of retirement is creeping upwards in most countries as governments try to balance pensions and stretched public finances. But while many governments want us to work until we are 67, the age that people are actually retiring is often lower than you might think. Using the latest OECD data (unless specified) we reveal the countries that actually work the longest.

South Africa: 60

South Africans retire at 60, on average, according to South Africa Government Services. The government doesn't impose an official age as such, so it is left to employees to liaise with employers to find an 'agreed' age of retirement.

France: 60.55

In France, women on average retire at 60.6 years old, which is just a little later than men who typically retire at 60.5 years old. This is below the official retirement age of 62, but that was a recent increase. That said, the age when you can receive the full state pension amount is actually five years later, at 67, as the French government wants to encourage people to work later.

Greece: 60.7

On average Greek men retire just after they turn 61, while Greek women stop working just before they reach 60 years old. So it's not surprising that Greece sparked protests by raising its official retirement age to 67 in 2017, a two-year increase to the official retirement age for men and a staggering five-year rise for women. It was part of a cost-cutting drive after the country was bailed out by other European countries. Some voters elsewhere in Europe resented helping the Greek government when many of its citizens were drawing pensions in their 50s.

Belgium: 60.9

Belgian men and women retire officially at 65, but most people actually retire several years before through early retirement schemes, and the average effective age for men is 61.7 years old, while women tend to leave work just after they turn 60. The country's historically-generous state pension scheme was shaken up in 2011, when the early retirement age was increased to 62 and workers were forced to contribute for 40 years. The official pension age will rise to 66 from 2025 and 67 from 2030, measures which have proved highly unpopular, with strikes and protests across the country.

Poland: 61.35

Bucking the global trend, the Polish government recently slashed its retirement age from 67 to 65 for men and 60 for women. The move by the right-wing Law and Justice Party proved popular with voters as the last government had increased the retirement age in 2012. The new retirement age reflects reality as most male Poles actually work until they are 62.7, whereas Polish women already stop work at 60 on average.

Italy: 61.7

The average age men retire in Italy is just after their 62nd birthday, while women work until they are 61. But officially Italian men can retire at 66 years and 7 months and women a year earlier. A previous government tried to save money by proposing people retire at 67 in 2011. But most recently the coalition of the anti-establishment Five Star Movement and far-right League Party controversially reversed the planned increase. The retirement age will now be lowered to 62 for people who have paid into the Italian pension system for at least 38 years.

Spain: 61.9

The official retirement age in Spain is being gradually increased from 65 to 67 by 2027, but on average Spaniards are taking retirement at 61.9 (men at 62.2 and women at 61.6). The government had been under pressure from investors and international bodies to keep people working longer to cut public spending. Unions threatened to strike over the rise, but caved in after the government said workers could still retire at 65 if they had at least 38 years of contributions.

Netherlands: 63.25

Men and women in the Netherlands can currently give up work at 66, but the real average age Dutch people leave work is lower at 63.25 years old (63.8 years for men, and 62.7 for women). Despite this, the government is set to gradually increase the retirement age to 67 in 2021, amid concern over the costs of an ageing population. The government is also trying to incentivise citizens to work longer, with higher contributions for those still employed above pension age and bonuses for employers who hire them.

Finland: 63.45

Finnish men and women are encouraged to draw their pension from just after their 65th birthday, and there are big incentives to retire as late as 68. However, the rules let them retire earlier from 63, and with an average retirement age of 63.8 for men and 63.1 for women a lot of Finns are making the most of this opportunity.

Germany: 63.5

German men and women can currently draw their pension at 65, though the average German stops working at 63.5. The retirement age is 65 for people born before 1947, 67 for anyone born after 1964 and somewhere in the middle on a rising scale for people born in between. Politicians have even considered increasing the retirement age to 69 in decades to come in a bid to manage Germany's ageing population. So far there are no concrete plans to do so.

Denmark: 63.7

The official age Danish men and women can retire is 65, but this is due to gradually increase to 67 by 2022. After that, the retirement age will be linked to increases in life expectancy. In reality, the average Dane leaves the workplace at age 63.7, meaning that they are retiring more than a year before they can benefit from Denmark's pension scheme, the world's best according to Melbourne Mercer's Pension Index.

China: 64

In China the average age of retirement is 64 years old. This is nearly 10 years later than the official age, which is 50 for women and 60 for men, with citizens able to receive their full entitlement at the age of 55. With people working later and later into old age, there are concerns younger generations may not be able to find work. There are plans to raise the retirement age gradually for both men and women to 65 by 2045.

UK: 64.5

The retirement age in the UK is currently 65, and most work until a few months before they can draw their pension, with the average real retirement age at 64.5. Women saw a controversially steep rise in their pension age from 60 to 65

in the last three years. Both sexes currently face a gradual hike to 66 by October 2020, and another rise to 68 by 2039 at the latest.

Argentina: 64.5

Argentine men can currently retire at 65 and women at 60, though on average most retire at 64.5, as long as they have at least 30 years of contributions and service. A plan to increase the pension age to 70 for men and 63 for women sparked violent protests in 2017 but was passed by lawmakers. The government also proposed people should carry on working as long as necessary to reach the 30-year threshold. Argentina's President Mauricio Macri hoped to cut public spending to win the support of foreign investors.

Canada: 64.75

Canadians can draw a means-tested state pension from 65, as long as they have lived in the country for 40 years. The system is flexible though, with workers able to take less money from 60 or an increased pension if they delay it until their late 60s. The average age isn't too far off the recommended age, with people retiring at 64.75, which works out at 66 for men and 63.5 for women. The previous government had planned to delay retirement until 67 from 2023, but current Prime Minister Justin Trudeau scrapped the measure.

Norway: 64.75

Norway's state pension age has been 67 for men and women since the 1970s, but most men stop working at the age of 65.4 and women even earlier at 64.1. Nowadays the retirement age is flexible for earnings-related pensions, which Norwegians can draw from as early as their 62nd birthday. There are no plans to raise the retirement age any higher.

Australia: 64.9

The Australian government has recently increased the official pension age: people born before 1952 can retire at 65, but those born after that face gradual increases until it reaches 67 in 2023. The Liberal Party had tried to increase the retirement age to 70, but other parties shied away from an even bigger hike. But when do they actually retire? Australians have retired much later at 64.9.

Switzerland: 65

In Switzerland, the average retirement age is 65.7 for men and 64.3 for women, which combined makes an average of 65. This is in line with the official retirement age of 65 for men and 64 for women. However, the Swiss state pension offers a flexible pension age, and pensions can be drawn much earlier but with lower entitlements, or up to five years later with much bigger payments.

Romania: 65

The average retirement age in Romania is 65 years old, according to the National Revenue Agency. This matches the official age for Romanian men who can draw their pension from 65, while women can draw it four years earlier, and some mothers even earlier if they meet certain criteria. However, the retirement age for women is set to gradually increase to 63 years by 2030, and recent reforms have set the minimum contribution at 15 years, and the full contribution threshold at 35 years. The reforms reflected fears about the inadequate size of the country's pension pot. High unemployment, significant emigration and widespread early retirement in the 1990s left Romania struggling to balance the books.

Ireland: 65.1

Men and women in Ireland can both draw their pension from 66, with most men retiring once they turn 66, while women leave work earlier at the age of 64.2 on average. The retirement age is due to rise to 68 from 2028, one of the highest in the world. The government also recently increased the compulsory age at which civil servants retire from 65 to 70 allowing those in the role to work longer if they wish.

Sweden: 65.65

Swedish people can draw their means-tested state pension at 61 via the country's flexible earnings-related scheme, although the guaranteed pension age is 65. However, the lowest pension age is due to rise to 64 and to 67 for the guaranteed pension by 2026. This will likely only have a limited impact on many Swedes though, as the average age people leave the workplace is already 65.

Turkey: 66

Turkey's official retirement age is 60 for men and 58 for women, but most work beyond that until 66. The pension age is gradually rising to 65 for both men and women by 2044 at the latest. Turkey's system actually allows for people who started contributing to a pension in the late 1970s and have at least 25 years of payments to retire at 44 should they choose.

USA: 66.85

The average American retirement age is 67.6 for men and 66.1 for women, but the rules vary depending on citizens' age. Anyone born before 1938 can retire at 65, while those born after 1959 have to work until they are 67. The retirement age increases gradually up to 67 for those born in-between. Many Americans over 65 switch to part-time work rather than leaving the workforce altogether.

Portugal: 67.6

On average Portuguese men retire at 69.6 years old, while women leave work at 65.6. Officially men and women can both expect to retire at 66 years and 3 months, though this will increase to 67 in 2029. The age increased in 2017 because of rising life expectancy and pressure to save money after Portugal received an international bailout in 2011.

Israel: 67.8

On average people in Israel work until they are just shy of 68, with men working until they are almost 70 and women 65.7. This is higher than the official ages set by the government, which says men should retire at 67 and women at 62. Politicians voted to increase women's retirement age over a decade ago but have been reluctant to make the proposal a reality, according to the Haaretz newspaper.

Iceland: 68.2

Icelandic men and women have some of the longest life expectancies on the planet, but have long had to work until they are 67. Research suggests Icelanders tend to save effectively for retirement, unlike many other countries. However, most men actually stop working only shortly before their 70th birthday, and women at 66.6, meaning that on average Icelanders work longer than they officially have to.

New Zealand: 68.4

There is no official retirement age in New Zealand, but pension payments start at the age of 65. On average both men and women are working beyond that age, with women leaving work just before they turn 67 and men nearly working to their 70th birthday. There are plans to raise the pension age to 67 in the late 2030s. The residency rules to qualify for a state pension are also expected to change, with pensioners required to have lived in the country for at least 20 years, rather than 10 as previously.

Mexico: 69

Mexico's retirement age is 65 for men and women, but early retirement is possibly from 60. However, in reality the average age people leave the workplace is much higher at 69. Why? Workers need to have paid in for about 24 years to receive a pension, but less than a third of the working population is expected to qualify, as many are in casual work and have not made enough, or any, contributions. Anyone who has not paid in enough gets the money back as one lump sum instead.

Japan: 69.95

Perhaps it's not surprising that Japan's citizens work until they're nearly 70 on average, as their life expectancy is among the highest in the world and the country already has one of the oldest populations. Citizens are actually allowed to draw their pension at the age of 62, but men often work past the age of 70 and women until the age of 69.3. Now the government plans to let people delay drawing their pension until their 70s in a bid to save money and keep people in work longer.

South Korea: 73

South Korea comes in with the longest working life of exactly 73 years. Both men and women work on average 13 years longer than the official retirement age of 60. Why? The country is known for its long life expectancies, but also its poverty. Almost half of its citizens aged over 65 now live in relative poverty, which means that they may have to keep working later into their lives.

4 October 2019

The above information is reprinted with kind permission from Love Money.
© 2020 lovemoney.com

www.lovemoney.com

Lowering the state pension age for women won't create four million jobs for young people

By Pippa Allen-Kinross

Claim

Lowering the state pension age for women back to 60 would create four million jobs for the younger generation.

A Facebook post shared 22,000 times claims that four million job vacancies would be created for young people if the state pension age for women was lowered back to 60. This is not accurate.

The post says: '4 million job vacancies could be created for the younger generation in one fell swoop, by moving 50s women pension back to 60.' The post seems to attribute this to 'Sue Walker', but it is not clear who she is.

The state pension age for women is a subject of much controversy. The Pensions Act 1995 said the age women are entitled to a state pension should be raised from 60 to 65 over a 10-year period to April 2020. This timetable was accelerated in the Pensions Act 2011, so that it reached 65 in November 2018 and will increase to 66 by October 2020, before rising alongside the state pension age for men until both reach 68. We've written about the timetable for changes before.

This means that many women born in the 1950s are retiring later than expected. An often-cited figure is that 3.8 million women were affected by this change.

Full Fact contacted the House of Commons Library to check this figure, which told us that in 2017 it estimated that almost 3.8 million women (3,777,000) were born between 6 April 1950 and 5 April 1960 and would be affected by the Pensions Act 1995. Of these, 2.72 million women were born on or after 6 April 1953 and affected by the 2011 Act. (The House of Commons Library has since revised these estimates to 3.72 million women and 2.68 million women respectively).

The Facebook post's mention of four million jobs may be in reference to the 3.7 million women who were impacted by the initial rise of the state pension age, although there is no evidence that all of these women are currently employed and many will have reached state pension age already.

Employment figures from the Office for National Statistics (ONS), covering the period from April to June 2020, showed that more than five million women over the age of 50 are in employment (4,497,079 women aged 50-64 and 564,401 women aged 65 or over).

This data does not include a metric just for women over the age of 60, so it is not possible to give a concrete figure for the number of women over 60 in employment. However, population figures from the ONS put the total number of women aged 60-69 in the UK at 3.65 million, making it very unlikely that four million women over 60 and not already eligible for the state pension are currently employed.

The number of people in jobs and the number of jobs won't be exactly the same, because some people work more than one job, but figures from 2019 suggest there aren't enough people over 60 working second jobs for this to make a significant difference.

There is also no certainty that all would take the opportunity to retire if the state pension age was lower, or that their jobs would be available to the younger generation.

20 August 2020

Conclusion

This is not accurate. There is no evidence that four million women over the age of 60 are currently employed nor that they would all retire given the opportunity.

The above information is reprinted with kind permission from Full Fact.
© 2010 - 2020 Full Fact

www.fullfact.org

'It was a case of heat or eat': Seven women explain why they want pension age dropped to 60

'I cannot go out or use my gas as I cannot afford the cost. I live on bread and jam. I watch TV in the dark as I am frightened of having my electricity turned off, again,' says Julia Holland, 65.

By Maya Oppenheim, Women's Correspondent

Almost four million women were affected by the controversial state pension age rise from 60 to 66 for women born after March 1950 – with the United Nations previously warning they are at increased risk of 'poverty, homelessness and financial hardship'.

While BackTo60, a campaign group calling for full restitution for women hit by the state pension increase, lost its landmark High Court battle after taking the government to court over the pension hike, they are appealing the ruling on Tuesday.

The Independent spoke to women up and down the country who have been directly impacted by the state pension overhaul.

Pamela Satchwell, who lives just outside of Blackpool, said she was pushed into destitution and lost her home due to the state pension age rising.

The 66-year-old, who previously worked as a civil servant and then as a teacher, said the Covid-19 emergency had wreaked havoc with her mental health and worsened pre-existing agoraphobia.

'My husband had an accident. I had to stop working to look after him for years. He died in 2013. He had a massive heart attack. I came down and found him. I still can't get rid of the picture in my mind. I felt really lost. I panicked. I'd already lost a father six months previously and my mother a few years previously. I'm an only child. I have no relations. I haven't even got a next of kin. When my husband died suddenly, I was left with the mortgage and a lot of debt I couldn't manage.

'It was a case of heat or eat. I ended up going to the food bank. In the end, I couldn't pay the mortgage so the mortgage company made me sell my house. I even had to sell the bits of jewellery my husband bought me to buy food and electric. Sometimes, I've thought it would be easier if I wasn't here. Coronavirus has made life harder. I can't see an end to this. I'm stuck in a flat. I have arthritis. I suffer from panic attacks and agoraphobia. I feel the four walls are holding me up. I'm extremely stressed. I'm not sleeping. I'm frightened to go to the doctor as I don't want to get the virus. I'm on antidepressant tablets and high blood pressure tablets. I have absolutely no confidence.'

Sheila Jones, who lives in the Midlands, said she had been caught up in the pension age rise twice but only learnt about the change by going onto the HMRC website.

The 66-year-old, who was an intensive care and clinical research nurse until she retired last June, said she had to go through two knee operations and needed to go part-

time, but this was not financially feasible due to having a mortgage to pay and no state pension to rely on.

'I was never told. I never got a letter. I had to sell my house in London and now I'm renting. It had devastating effects. I had my future mapped out. I'm not having the life I had planned for myself. If you add it up, it's tens of thousands of pounds I lost. As it goes on, it is more and more stress. My situation is much more uncertain than it should have been. I worked very hard. When you think about the injustice, it rises like bile in your system. I feel very bitter we were treated that way. I will not give up. This is an injustice.

'My life was detrimentally changed by the government and therefore out of my control. This has affected me mentally and seeing the effects in other women my age is very upsetting. I've got a friend who is a teacher in her early sixties who is having to work until she is 66. She is wondering how she is going to manage. I am very hopeful and positive about the court case. I'm looking to forward to getting our case heard again and hoping for justice.'

Julia Jacobs, who lives in Solihull, says she was dependent on her state pension due to spending most of her adult life bringing up four children and project-managing properties she bought with her former husband.

The 60-year-old was working as a part-time exam invigilator on a zero hour contract prior to the Covid-19 emergency but is now living off life savings due to not getting any support or furlough pay from the government.

'I probably won't get a job as I'm 60. I really needed the security of my state pension at this time in my life. I won't get my state pension until 2025. The state age rise has made me feel devalued as a human being by society. Why are we women being punished so much when we didn't have the benefits of equal opportunity throughout life?

'I'm feeling extremely nervous and agitated about the court case. I hope we'll win. I can't handle another knockback for all the other 1950s women who are in much more dire straits than myself. Some are contemplating suicide because there is no future. They have lost so much. Some women are walking the breadline. The damage to their financial, emotional and physical health is tragic. These women should be retired. Some are working in factories, cleaning hospitals or people's homes, some as teachers, some as teaching assistants. We're talking about jobs that are high risk in a pandemic.'

Frances Neil, who lives in southeast Essex, said she was only notified of the state pension age rise around 18 months before she turned 60.

The 66-year-old, a former primary school headteacher who is a mother-of-four, said it was initially hiked up to 63 but then when she reached that age it was again moved up to 65.

'The state pension age rise is unfair and unjust in every conceivable way. I was the only carer for my elderly and frail parents so couldn't devote as much time to their care as I hoped and wanted. They did suffer as a result and so did I. My husband became disabled and I couldn't support him as I intended and wished, either. All this, on top of running a large primary school, was a huge emotional, professional and financial burden. I wanted to retire to care for and spend time with family members and support our children with childcare too, so they could work, but was caught having to remain at work and watch those I loved suffer when I could have done much more for them.

'My health has suffered irreparably as a result of the accumulative stress and led to me retiring before I received my state pension age, even though I knew financially I would lose some state pension. I received no notice so I could plan my financial affairs. The DWP never thought women would fight or be heard. Well, we have and have been heard and will continue to fight for our cause. This is another example of women bearing the brunt of financial 'belt-tightening'. Many women are not financially secure or independent, particularly those of my generation.'

Patricia Hamzahee said the state pension age hike had not personally affected her as she wants to carry on working because she does not have a physically strenuous job.

But the 61-year-old, who works in social impact investing and lives in southwest London, said the rise has been a massive blow for other women of a similar age to her.

'If they had plans to retire at a certain age that is what they planned for and that is what they saved for. That is what they organised their lives around. If all of a sudden I had been told I had to work longer but wasn't planning to, I would be aggrieved. You are told all of the time by authoritative voices – whether that is the government or financial advisors – to plan for your retirement. That was drilled into me when I was young. So when the rug is pulled out from under you, through no fault of your own, that undermines your efforts to plan. I hope they win the court case because I think it is unfair.'

Joan Hughes, who is not retired due to her state pension age rising to 63 initially and then again to 66, has been unable to find suitable work since reaching the age of 60 in spite of being well qualified and experienced in both childcare and office administration.

The 63-year-old, who lives in Milton Keynes and is currently unemployed, said she had previously found part-time work at a nursery on a minimum wage, zero hour contract, but injured her hip and knee after being expected to carry out the same heavy physical duties as staff a third of her age.

'Without a proper income, I have had to live very frugally indeed. I had to give up my car. I have a heart condition and arthritis. Not only has my physical health been affected, I am also under treatment for depression. Constant high levels of anxiety have resulted in disrupted sleep patterns, panic attacks and loss of confidence, a situation made worse by the Covid-19 lockdown, which has meant my life has become even more limited and isolated.

'It is the final insult to now expect me either to work in low-paid, menial, insecure employment for another six years or else continue claiming unemployment benefit. I have brought up my daughter on my own. I have looked after sick parents on my own. There is a stigma attached to being unemployed. It is deeply demoralising. I think it is cruel to saddle me with this hopeless, humiliating future for six years.

'The impending court case has made me feel anxious. I think the case for full restitution of pension rights is fair and reasonable, however, there are large sums of money at stake and I'm afraid this will influence what is considered fair and reasonable. I think the judgement will be as much about how women are valued in society as anything else and my experiences of this have so far not been good.'

Julia Holland, an unemployed visual merchandiser who lives in Newcastle upon Tyne, said she was suffering severe hardship due to the state pension age rising.

The 65-year-old said she has to choose between eating or heating and cannot afford the bus fare to travel around.

'I left school at 16, went straight into a job, married at 22, had my son at 28. Because my son was not very well at birth and then had to have several operations, I had to leave my job. So I stayed at home nursing my son for nearly five years. My husband continued to work and contribute to his pension. From then on I was in and out of work, sometimes full-time, sometimes part-time, so never did get the opportunity to fill up my pension pot.

'Then my son died in his sleep. Since then my life has been so hard financially, as well as mentally. Trying to handle things on my own, trying to support myself. So at 65, I still have some months to go before I can retire, but I have had enough. If I could have retired when I thought I could, life would have been a little easier, to say the least. I had no time to prepare for the robbery that took place. I am now going from one temp job to the next on a minimum wage. At the moment I am on universal credit. I cannot go out or use my gas as I cannot afford the cost. I live on bread and jam. I watch TV in the dark as I am frightened of having my electricity turned off, again. The rise in the state pension was unfair as I did not have adequate time to prepare for this. I am excited that this case will see justice is done and I am positive we will win.'

19 July 2020

The above information is reprinted with kind permission from *The Independent*.
© independent.co.uk 2020

www.independent.co.uk

Over 8m over-50s doubt they have enough for retirement

By Kevin Rose

Research from over 50s finance provider SunLife suggests that more than seven million over-50s have no private pension and more than eight million don't think they have enough money to fund their retirement.

In its *Finances After 50* study, SunLife found that 28% of over-50s do not have a private or company pension.

The number of people over 50 in the UK is now more than 25 million, according to the ONS, which indicates that around seven million over-50s across the UK have no private pension savings.

SunLife's research shows that women over 50 are less likely to have a private pension than men of the same age – more than a third of women surveyed said they didn't have a private pension (35%) – which across the UK is around 4.6 million. Of the men surveyed, one in five said they didn't (20%), which is equivalent to around 2.4 million men across the UK.

The study also found that a third of over-50s – which equates to 8.3 million – say they don't think they have enough money to provide them with sufficient income for their retirement with women more worried about not having enough money in later life than men.

Just 13% of women over 50 say they are confident they will have enough money for a retirement income; 36% don't think they will have enough, which across the UK is around 4.7 million women. In contrast, 22% of men over 50 say they are confident they have enough and 30% (equivalent to around 3.6 million) say they don't.

Many over-50s say they will look to other income sources other than pensions for retirement income; 27% say they are hoping their partner or spouse's pension will fund their retirement, rising to 30% of women, 12% say they are going to continue to work to provide an income, while 11% are expecting an inheritance to cover it, which suggests 2.7 million people over 50 are relying on being left money to fund their retirement.

Simon Stanney, equity release director at SunLife, said: 'Pensions Awareness Week is all about raising awareness of pensions and the importance of retirement planning, but we can see from our research that many of those nearing retirement have concerns that they are not ready.

'Obviously, the sooner you start saving into a pension, the better, but it is never too late. However, the older you are, the more you'll need to put aside each month to build up that pot for retirement. We have a number of blogs on our site written by finance experts offering help and advice to people who have retired or are nearing retirement including What to do if you haven't saved enough for retirement and How to make money in retirement.

'For those who are worried that they will struggle to build up enough of a pension pot to fund their retirement, looking to property wealth could be a viable option.'

SunLife's research shows that on average, homeowners over 50 have seen their homes increase in value by £127,316 over the past 20 years.

Stanney added: 'Downsizing is an option for many, however, our SunLife research shows that most over 50s don't want to move, and this is where equity release could offer a solution. It allows homeowners over 55 to release some of the money tied up in the value of their home without having to move. Exploring Equity Release is a series of blogs, articles, tools and guides to help you work out if equity release is right for you and if so, how much equity you could release.'

14 September 2020

The above information is reprinted with kind permission from Best Advice.
© 2020 Trek Publishing Limited

www.bestadvice.co.uk

The number of older workers is increasing fast, yet they face growing age discrimination

Older women are more likely to be rejected for jobs than older men, and less likely to be called for another interview than women under 45, writes Allyson Zimmermann.

The days of collecting your carriage clock and waving goodbye to your workmates of 45 years are over, particularly as more people, whether through choice or necessity, are now working into their late 60s and 70s. In the EU, about one fifth (19%) of the population is 65 or more. A 65-year-old in the United Kingdom can now expect to live for another 23 years, almost 10 years longer than in 1948. And in the not-too-distant future, retirees in Europe will outnumber the working-age population, despite efforts to raise the retirement age.

The average retirement age for men and women across Europe is currently 65, but Spain, Germany and France plan to increase the age to 67. While in the UK, there are plans to increase the retirement age to 68. Yet, while the fastest growing labour pool is older workers, these workers are also reporting a rise in age discrimination. Ageism is now the most common type of discrimination in Europe.

It cuts both ways for older and younger workers, but older workers are most likely to report complaints of ageism. In Europe, 44% of older workers, and 64% in the UK, said they were concerned about age discrimination. Both older men and women report biases in the workplace, particularly relating to their ability and performance. They report being seen as less innovative, less able to adapt and less qualified than younger members of staff; they suffer in a working culture that favours younger employees.

These issues are even more dire for older women, who also face a gender pay gap penalty. Women experience ageism from around the age of 40 in the UK, compared with men who experience it from 45. Older women can feel marginalised and pressured, for instance, to adhere to gendered youthful beauty standards. For example, women are reportedly more likely to dye their hair to cover any grey, than men. Older women are also more likely to be rejected for jobs than older men; and are twice as likely to not be called back for another interview than women under 45. In the United States, from 2007 to 2013, the unemployment rate for older women (over 65) jumped from 14% to 50%. This is despite studies revealing how older employees positively contribute to companies financially and culturally including:

♦ the benefits of holding onto more talent and experience;

♦ the importance of mutual training and swapping of experience between older and younger individuals, which can support better decision-making and increased productivity and innovation;

♦ cost savings from retaining older employees rather than hiring new talent;

♦ and a happier team as older individuals tend to report higher job satisfaction levels.

A 2013 study from Zwick, Göbel and Fries also showed that mixed-age teams in the workplace are more productive than

teams of workers all the same age. Simply put, companies that discriminate against segments of the population from accessing work they're qualified to do will lose out in the 'war for talent'.

Catalyst research has found that people who are not truly embraced as part of a team can feel excluded and are prohibited from advancing within the organisation. Companies may have started to look at age as a diversity issue, with recent efforts mostly focused on the millennial generation, who are estimated to make up around half the workforce, but how are they addressing older generations in diversity efforts? By ignoring older workers as a dimension of diversity, organisations are losing knowledge, skills and experience. A study by PwC estimates that OECD (Organization for Economic Cooperation and Development) members could increase their total GDP by around $3.5 trillion by following New Zealand's example of having one of the highest employment rates in the world for older workers (55 and over).

How can organisations sell to the marketplace if they do not represent them? Visa reported in 2016 that people over 50 represent more than half of U.S. consumer spending; products and services for this growing segment of the population will be a rich source of future market growth.

It is time for the corporate world to treat ageism against older workers as they would any form of prejudice, based on negative stereotypes and myths. Age, like gender, does not predict a worker's value. Bias is holding older workers back and needs to be removed from the workplace. Organisations that value older workers' contribution and experience, and do not see them as 'past their sell-by date', could be unlocking a key to their future prosperity in the 21st century.

8 February 2020

This article was originally published in LSE Business Review.

The above information is reprinted with kind permission from the London School of Economics and Political Science (LSE). © LSE 2020

www.blogs.lse.ac.uk

How biscuits enriched with protein could keep the UK's ageing population strong

An article from *The Conversation*.

By Alex Johnstone, Personal Chair in Nutrition, The Rowett Institute, University of Aberdeen and Madeleine Myers, Research Assistant, University of Aberdeen

The world's ageing populations are increasing every year. In 2016, 18% of the UK's population was aged 65 years or older – by 2046, this group will account for nearly a quarter of the people living in the British Isles.

Add to this the fact that normal ageing is associated with a gradual decline in muscle mass, known as sarcopenia which can impair muscle function and strength, it is crucial, now and in the future, to prolong people's health span and their ability to be active and live independently. For that we need to understand the role of dietary intake of protein to promote healthy and active ageing.

New evidence suggests that current dietary recommendations for protein intake may be insufficient to achieve this goal and that individuals might benefit by increasing their intake and frequency of consumption of high-quality protein.

From the third decade of life we begin to lose muscle mass and, scarily, losses of between 30 to 50% have been reported between the ages of 40 and 80. Loss of muscle function and strength reduces the ability to perform everyday tasks and also increases the risk of falling.

So what can we do about it? Current UK dietary recommendations for protein intake in adults is set at 0.75g/kg of body weight per day regardless of age. But international recommendations specifically for older people vary between 1.2 and 1.5g/kg/day – although these do not take account for physical activity level. From mid-life onwards, adults may benefit from a greater intake of protein to slow the ageing of muscles.

Looking at the current UK intake of protein, there seem to be key areas for improvement:

1. Protein amount: The amount of protein intake tends to decline with age, partially due to what is called anorexia of ageing, which happens when older people don't eat regularly enough. The latest National Diet and Nutrition Survey (NDNS) data indicates that one in three of over-40s do not meet the lower UK target of protein intake, and more

than 80% fail to meet the international recommendations for healthy ageing.

2. Distribution of protein intake: Consumption of two to three meals or snacks each containing 25 to 30g protein throughout the day is required for muscles to function at their best. However, estimates of protein intake in adults in mid-life indicate protein-rich meals tend to be eaten towards the end of the day, at lunch or dinnertime.

3. Type of protein: In the UK the main source of protein in the diet is from animal sources such as meat, dairy and fish. Increasing intake of plant-based proteins such as pulses, cereal products and nuts might be a more sustainable dietary pattern.

Taking the biscuit

Our research is part of the Protein For Life project, a recent partnership between academia and industry which aims to address the issue of declining muscle function due to malnutrition.

As part of this project, higher-protein biscuits were formulated containing different amounts of protein – either 12% or 20% of total energy coming from protein. To put this in perspective, a typical digestive biscuit has around 6% of total energy coming from protein. Products were also enriched with different sources of protein: animal protein (whey powder) or plant protein (peanut butter, soya and wheat crispies). Higher-protein biscuits offer a handy on-the-go snack which can top up protein anywhere, at any time, and help spread intake throughout the day.

According to current legislation for front-of-pack labelling, these products could also be labelled as a "source of protein" or "high in protein" for the 12% and 20% protein biscuits respectively, alerting consumers to their "protein power".

A group of older adults (40 and upwards) took part in a blind test to find out which biscuit (and therefore level of protein enrichment) was preferred, and whether they tasted good. Biscuit tasting at the trial site in Aberdeen (one of four across the UK) revealed that the source-of-protein biscuits (12%) were favoured over the high-protein biscuits (20%). This suggests that consumers might favour a more subtle approach to reformulating much-loved products with extra protein.

Although members of the test group were divided over the type of protein used, more indicated that they generally prefer plant over animal sources of protein. This potentially identifies a niche for food products enriched with plant proteins specifically, which would help to reduce the environmental impact of the protein-enriched biscuit.

From our research into the use of plant proteins to support healthy ageing, we have created a framework for action that explains clearly the issues facing the elderly – and what can be done by the government, the food industry and consumers themselves.

Our study raises important points about how the foods we eat affect our long-term health and our environment. Enriching biscuits with protein is a simple and easy way to ensure older people keep their protein levels at a constant level. It could help contribute to prolonged health and independence, and crucially, mean a better quality of life in old age.

25 September 2019

The above information is reprinted with kind permission from The Conversation
© 2010-2019, The Conversation Trust (UK) Limited

www.theconversation.com

Signs of old age appear much earlier in poorer people

Differences between the highest and lowest wealth groups were significant in numerous areas, including walking speed and memory.

By Paul Gallagher

Signs of old age appear much earlier in poorer people, a study has found. UCL researchers used a sample of more than 5,000 people, with an average age of 64, from the English Longitudinal Study of Ageing, first assessing them in 2004 and then eight years later in 2012.

They looked at whether the rate at which the participants aged varied with their socioeconomic status, and measured the rate of physical and mental decline in six areas including physical capability, such as hand grip strength and walking speed, memory and other functions, and emotional wellbeing.

Factors such as ethnicity, educational attainment, childhood socioeconomic status, and each person's number of long-term conditions such as arthritis, asthma, cancer, coronary heart disease, and diabetes, were taken into account.

The study found that there was a more rapid deterioration in physical, mental and social function among less wealthy people across all areas, patterns which could not be attributed to differences in health status.

Researchers looked at whether the rate at which the participants aged varied with their socioeconomic status

Biggest differences

The differences between the highest and lowest wealth groups were significant in numerous areas, with reductions in gait speed over the measured period 38 per cent greater in the lowest than in the highest wealth category, and around a 10 per cent difference in the decline in memory between the highest and lowest categories.

Lead author Professor Andrew Steptoe said: "'We know that people of lower socioeconomic status are at increased risk of

Definitions

Loneliness and social isolation are linked but distinct concepts.

Loneliness is a subjective, unwelcome feeling of lack or loss of companionship. It happens when we have a mismatch between the quantity and quality of social relationships that we have, and those that we want.

Social isolation is a more objective measure of the number of contacts and social interactions a person has.

disease in older age, but it has not been clear whether they are also at risk of a faster decline in age-related function not directly related to health conditions.

"What this study suggests is that independently of the state of health, there is faster decline of a wide range of age-related factors among less affluent people, adding to the evidence showing the corrosive nature of lower socioeconomic status on our bodies, our minds, and our capabilities."

The study is published in the *Proceedings of the National Academy of Sciences of the United States of America (PNAS).*

15 June 2020

The above information is reprinted with kind permission from iNews.
© 2020 JPIMedia Ltd.

www.inews.co.uk

Loneliness and social isolation in later life

Loneliness is not, and should not be, an inevitable part of getting older. However, many older people do experience loneliness and social isolation, which are linked to a range of health problems.

Who is at risk?

♦ Loneliness can occur at any point in life, and its intensity can vary across the life course.

♦ Risk of loneliness is not driven by age, but by people's circumstances.

♦ Older people might experience a number of circumstances that can increase the risk of loneliness and social isolation.

Barriers

♦ Some older people are reluctant to join groups explicitly targeting loneliness, groups that are dominated by one gender and groups that target older people only.

♦ Older LGBT people may be at risk of loneliness as they are more likely to be single, live alone and have lower levels of contact with relatives.

♦ Older people from ethnic minority groups may experience 'overlooked' loneliness due to language barriers, poverty, and assumptions that they live in 'traditional' family structures that prevent loneliness.

What works

Some promising approaches to reducing loneliness and social isolation include:

♦ Supporting people to remain engaged with activities and interests they enjoy, and that are meaningful to them.

♦ Designing mixed-generational groups that mirror social interactions in everyday life.

♦ Offering befriending services for those who would prefer them to group activities.

♦ Promoting an active role for older people in the development and running of activities, and opportunities to volunteer.

♦ Addressing underlying psychological factors related to socialising such as expectations around social contact, social confidence and resilience.

Recommendations

♦ The Government must fully resource NHS England to support the commitments to social prescribing outlined in the NHS long term plan.

♦ The Government should take a whole-system approach to promote ways for people to maintain social connections and relationships across the life course, e.g. ensuring older people can access public transport, ensuring town centres are age-friendly.

♦ The Government should work with the Office for National Statistics to develop an appropriate tool to measure social isolation at different stages across the life course, similar to the work on a loneliness measure.

♦ The Government and employers should pilot interventions to support people at risk of becoming lonely in older age.

The above information is reprinted with kind permission from Independent Age and The Campaign to End Loneliness © 2020 Independent Age

www.independentage.org
www.campaigntoendloneliness.org

Loneliness and social isolation - now and in the future

6-13%

aged 65+
A fairly constant proportion (6–13%) of people aged 65+ report feeling lonely often or always

aged 65+
Nearly one in three who have experienced partner bereavement report being very lonely

aged 65+
In later life, loneliness is most common amongst the oldest in our society

3.4m 2008   **3.9m 2018**

aged 65+
In 2018, 3.9 million people aged 65+ were living alone in the UK, an increase of half a million people since 2008

As our population ages, the absolute number of lonely older people is likely to increase

Life circumstances
linked to loneliness and social isolation

Retirement

Poor physical and mental health

Bereavement

Poverty

Living alone

Caring for somebody

Impacts
of loneliness and social isolation

Loneliness:
- key risk factor for depression in older age
- linked with a 40% increased risk of dementia

Social isolation:
- strongly linked to cardiovascular disease

Loneliness, social isolation, and living alone are all associated with an increased risk of early death.

A million elderly people skipping meals because they find eating alone too lonely, charity reveals

By Gabriella Swerling

Almost a million elderly people are skipping meals or relying on ready meals because they find eating alone too lonely.

New research, commissioned by The Royal Voluntary Service (RVS) and published today, said that the loneliness epidemic among Britain's elderly community was to blame for these eating habits.

The charity found that 11% (or 955,464) people aged 70 and over in the UK confess to relying on ready meals and convenience foods to keep them fed with nearly a quarter (23%) saying they skip their daily meals at least three times a week.

Over one in five over 70s (22%) stated they ate all their daily meals alone each week, rising to over a quarter (26%) of people over 80. Of those who eat most of their meals alone, 38% admit they miss having company at meal times.

The study also found over one fifth (21%) cook less than four meals a week from scratch, with 17% saying they miss having someone to cook for (rising to 24% of females) and 8% saying they lost their desire to cook when their partner died.

Rebecca Kennelly, Director of Volunteering, Royal Voluntary Service, said: 'Our lunch club volunteers are just one shining example of how people can gift their time to support their local communities.

'For more than 80 years, Royal Voluntary Service has been mobilising volunteers to meet the big needs of the day, and as our research shows, one of the most pressing is helping people age better - specifically supporting them to eat more healthily and to experience the health and wellbeing benefits of eating with others.'

Researchers added that eating alone can have a negative impact on people's health with 41% of over 70s admitting they only sometimes follow a healthy diet.

Additionally, one in twenty (5%) often forget to eat, and the equivalent of 390,000 older people (5%) rely on cold foods such as sandwiches to keep them going.

The research was released alongside a new film starring TV presenter Rachel Riley, who visits a RVS Lunch club in Rickmansworth, Hertfordshire, to meet volunteers and witness how these clubs are providing older people with a chance to eat nutritious, hot meals in the company of others.

Rachel Riley said: 'Older people are often by themselves and it can be difficult to motivate yourself to make a nice hot meal. Loneliness is one of the worst things in terms of mental health and general wellbeing, so getting people together and having somewhere you can look forward to going to each week is fantastic.

The volunteers themselves get a lot out of it too because they get to know the people who come in every week.'

5 November 2019

The above information is reprinted with kind permission from *The Telegraph*.
© Telegraph Media Group Limited 2020

www.telegraph.co.uk

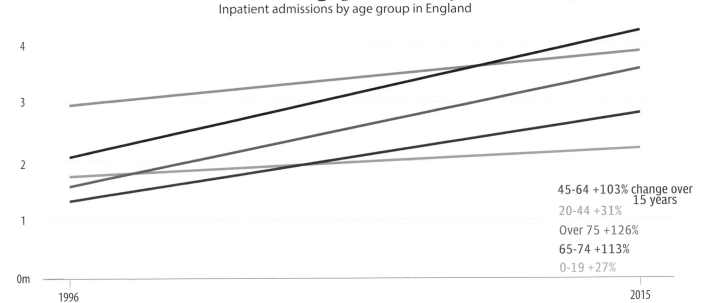

The NHS' burden is increasing - particularly from elderly people
Inpatient admissions by age group in England

45-64 +103% change over 15 years
20-44 +31%
Over 75 +126%
65-74 +113%
0-19 +27%

1996   2015

Source: IFS

media-fuelled obsession with self-image. But I also know plenty of middle-aged people who seem to have a sense of entitlement, and every generation likes to believe they are suffering more than any other.

Still, it really is hard for millennials. I bought my first house at age 43, a four-bedroom place in north London, through a shared ownership scheme. Some youngsters today may never be able to afford to buy or even find decent accommodation, unless their parents are rich enough to help them.

It's easy to rush to judgment of those like Nicole, who get stuck in the family home but appear to fritter their money away. Yet as our week together progressed, I discovered there was more to her than meets the eye. Through hard work she's built up her own business and is clearly skilled at what she does.

So while we taught her to throw away less and conserve more, she taught me plenty about how to use modern technology to achieve what you want to achieve. I don't have a product to market, but I am an activist and co-run a company that helps local people find money to start their own businesses, so I gratefully drew on Nicole's business sense when she gave me advice on the matter. We've stayed in touch ever since.

As I discovered during our week together, there's so much more to young people like her than is instantly apparent. Only a fool would underestimate young women who are using themselves in a very creative way to help sell their products and earn money. No, it's not something my generation is used to. But we shouldn't write them off or dismiss them. We have a lot to learn from the younger generation, just as they do from ours.

Since Nicole came to stay, we've started to look for a lodger to share our home rent-free in return for some help with the gardening. Perhaps if we really luck out, it will end up being a millennial."

Nicole Moukatas, 27

"I still live at home with my family: my mum, my mum's partner, my sister and brother.

Fortunately we all get along, and we all have learnt to understand each other's ways. We are a positive household and support each other's journey 100 per cent.

The problem is moving out isn't as straightforward as it used to be - something that's often forgotten by older generations, who wonder why we don't just grow up, get a house by a particular age and stop wasting money on other things.

I am on my own journey and I'm very happy with it, there's no right or wrong time when you should move out, have children, get married; you should be happy within yourself, and when you feel the time is right then do so. Everyone is on their own path, and that's OK.

I was planning on moving out this year but Covid-19 made things difficult. So next year it's the first thing I will be doing. To achieve this goal, I make sure I am always working hard and growing within myself. I run my own online women's clothing business, do modelling for a wholesale company (due to coronavirus I haven't returned yet) and also run a

speed-dating event every month. It's taken a few years to build up my company from scratch, and I've worked so hard to achieve what I've achieved so far, but I'm not even halfway to where I want to be yet.

I'm very grateful for my mother as living at home has helped me a lot with saving a deposit for a house. It would have been far more difficult if I'd had to move out and pay to rent somewhere in London and save money at the same time. It would have taken me much longer.

It was easier to buy your first home in the past. These days it's harder to strike out on your own, and I also think its important today to have more than one source of income. But that doesn't mean people of my age shouldn't continue to enjoy some of the finer things in life. I believe in working hard and treating myself by doing things that make me happy.

When I moved in with Claudine and Ted, they seemed shocked at how freely I spent money: £10 to £15 a day on my lunch at work, and about £150 a month on hair and beauty treatments alone. I like going out for nice meals with my friends, and prior to lockdown I would go to the gym, too. I also love nights in though, learning new things, sewing and reading.

I spend a limited time on social media promoting my business. This is a necessary part of the job, although older people seem to think my generation are obsessed with our phones. The fact is most of my customers come through Instagram. It's integral to what I do, not some pointless, time-wasting exercise.

After a few days of getting to know each other, Claudine came to appreciate that. But at first she did seem to struggle to see past my appearance. She mentioned my lashes, my hair and nails, all of which I take great care over. I think she may have thought I was therefore somehow superficial; but when we got to know each other, she told me looks didn't matter and affectionately called me her 'shiny face'.

As for me, I didn't have too many preconceptions of what her generation was like. She and Ted are older than my own parents (who are in their early 50s) but I got on with them like you would with a cool set of grandparents, and now they are my friends for life.

A four-decade age gap doesn't stop you connecting with someone, and our new friendship is proof of this. Since my brief stint as their housemate last year, I've visited them twice already, and we're constantly in touch online. They have taught me how to economise a bit and how to cut down on plastic.

The pandemic has set things back a little, but I'm now in the slow process of finally moving out and buying a place by myself. I'm ready to have my own space, not least in the wake of lockdown. I won't be staying in North London, I'll be looking further out or even somewhere abroad. I'm ready to go somewhere different, and start my next journey."

28 August 2020

The above information is reprinted with kind permission from *The Telegraph*.
© Telegraph Media Group Limited 2020

www.telegraph.co.uk

Social care crisis wastes nearly £30,000 of NHS money an hour

Age UK is calling for the future of social care to be put on a sustainable financial footing urgently.

By Jill Rennie, news editor at homecare.co.uk

A paucity of social care support is costing the NHS £587 million overall, equivalent to £640,000 every day, or £27,000 every hour. These figures are based on the 917 days between the last general election on 8 June 2017 and the upcoming election on 12 December 2019.

This is due to many people staying in hospital for longer than is clinically necessary. One of the major reasons for people being kept in hospital is because it is unsafe for them to go home as there is no social care support available for them. This is recorded by the hospital as a delayed day.

Staying in hospital is much more expensive than being supported at home or in a care home. It can also erode older people's confidence and lead to muscle wastage from staying in bed for long periods.

'We are all paying the price for the inability of our politicians to fix social care'

Caroline Abrahams, charity director of Age UK, said: 'It is appalling that two and a half million bed days will have been lost to the NHS between the last election and this one, simply because there is not nearly enough social care available to allow older people to be safely discharged.

'The waste of money this represents is staggering, coming in at more than half a billion pounds, but the human cost is arguably even greater, with many older people finding this means their recovery and rehabilitation is seriously delayed or in the worst cases put out of reach altogether.'

She added: 'We are all paying the price for the inability of our politicians to fix social care, whether you are waiting endlessly for a much-needed knee operation or facing hours of delay in A and E following an accident at home. When hospitals get jammed up because they can't discharge older people the effects feed right the way through and mean there are no beds for new patients who need them.'

The average number of people kept in hospital after they were ready to be discharged because of inadequate social care, was 2,750 every day, over the period between the last general election and this upcoming one.

98-year-old Mo can't be discharged as there is no care package in place

Age UK highlights the case of Mo, who is 98 and has been in hospital for five months after he had a stroke. The hospital told Mo he is ready to be discharged, but they are unable to do this because the social services team are understaffed and unable to put a care package in place.

The hospital is starting to suggest to Mo that he discharges himself without any care organised as this may be his only way to leave hospital and he is 'bed-blocking'.

Our social care system must be the government's 'number one policy priority'

Ms Abrahams said: 'We cannot go on treating the public in this way and leaving the NHS in an intolerably difficult situation. That's why it is imperative that whichever party forms the next government, it takes decisive action to rebuild our social care system and put it on an even financial keel. This ought to be its number one domestic policy priority.'

Sally Copley, director of Policy and Campaigns at Alzheimer's Society, called the figures from Age UK, 'compelling and indisputable evidence of the social care crisis gripping this country'.

She said: 'We hear tragic stories through our Fix Dementia Care campaign - a mother who spent years in hospital while being turned away from care home after care home, a woman who spent two months on a bed in a corridor because she couldn't get a care home place.

'Fixing this problem is not just the humane thing to do, it is the smart thing to do – it's clearly ridiculous to not address it when it is more expensive to keep a person with dementia in hospital than for them to get the care they need and deserve.'

5 Dec 2019

The above information is reprinted with kind permission from homecare.co.uk
© 2020 Tomorrow's Guides Ltd

www.homecare.co.uk

Do we really have to wait until we are 82 to find peak happiness?

By Helen Mead

As you grow older, it is tempting to think that you have left your happiest days behind.

The carefree days of your youth, when anything seemed possible, are worlds away, never to be relived.

Back then you had none of the restrictive trappings of later life - a mortgage, a job, others to provide for. And, most probably, you were fit and well. You had the rest of your life ahead.

I look back on my late teens and early twenties as the happiest years of my life so far, when I was a student, surrounded by friends and every day was fun and full of laughs.

But my happiest days could be yet to come - and a long way off. Experts say that our feelings of joy and contentment don't peak until the age of 82.

Leading neuroscientist Daniel Levitin says that older generations are much more cheerful than younger ones. The expert states that World Health Organisation data from 60 countries show that happiness grows with age.

He could be right. We tend to look at the past through rose coloured glasses. Come to think of it, the glory days of my late teens/early twenties were also full of insecurities.

Relationship woes were never far from the surface: will he/won't he call me? Does he/doesn't he like me? Will it/won't it last? At the time, it generated all sorts of worries.

Then there were all those exams, year after year.

And body image: Why does my hair look like a bird's nest? Why aren't my legs longer? Does my bum look big in this? Such things are far more burdensome at an age when you're trying to impress the opposite sex.

I probably felt happier back then because those things were all I had to worry about. But I wasn't in any way in control of my life.

Later, as we begin to take some sort of path, come the real worries - how to make a living. Jobs, mortgages, car loans, bills, bills, bills… And then, for many, children and the sometimes overwhelming, scary responsibility of supporting and raising a family, of keeping a roof over their head.

As Dr Levitin states in his book *The Changing Mind,* published this month, happiness declines in our 30s, but it starts to pick up once you reach 54.

I'm 59. I am certainly more settled than I was at 20 - I have a home, I have raised children who are now more-or-less self-sufficient, and, although I am no high flyer, I have built an enjoyable career.

But life still isn't a bed of roses. I still have a mortgage, alongside an insecure job and an uncertain future. I can't claim my pension for another eight years. Life is still throwing plenty of stress in my direction.

The thought of having to go through another 23 years of this before I feel complete contentment is depressing to say the least.

'You realise you've gotten through all these things that were stressing you out. If you make it to 82, you know you've managed, you're OK,' says Dr Levitin.

But will 82 really put me on cloud nine? I think it's more likely to put me in a care home. Those over 80 in good health should count themselves lucky.

I don't think true happiness is an age thing. Happiness is intermittent throughout life, appearing in fits and starts. It is, in my experience, about the little things: wine, food and a decent DVD on Saturday nights, walks in the countryside, time with family and friends, toasted teacake with a good cup of tea.

All these things bring pleasure.

But if we hit the ecstatic button at 82, then great. As I labour towards my eighties, I'll hang onto that thought.

24 February 2020

The above information is reprinted with kind permission from York Press.
© 2020 Newsquest Media Group Ltd

www.yorkpress.co.uk

Playing board games 'helps keep your memory sharp in old age'

Chess, bingo, cards and crosswords all help keep our minds agile, research suggests.

By Sabrina Barr

Playing board games may help elderly people keep their memories sharp, a study has claimed.

Those who regularly played games such as chess and bingo were more likely to have maintained their thinking skills, researchers found.

For the study, University of Edinburgh academics assessed 1,091 individuals, all of whom were born in 1939.

The participants' general cognitive function was noted at the age of 11 and 70, and then a series of cognitive tests were conducted at the ages of 70, 73, 76 and 79.

At the ages of 70 and 76, the respondents were asked how often they took part in activities such as playing cards, chess and bingo and crosswords.

Researchers then tried to determine if there was any link between the games they played and their cognitive abilities.

The study, which was published in *The Journals of Gerontology Series B: Psychological Sciences*, found that those who began playing more games in their later years were less likely to exhibit a decline in thinking skills.

This was made especially apparent with regards to the participant's memory function and thinking speed.

The researchers concluded that their findings could help establish what sorts of activities may benefit our cognitive abilities in old age.

Dr Drew Altschul, of the University of Edinburgh's School of Philosophy, Psychology and Language Sciences, explained: "For those in their 70s or beyond, another message seems to be that playing non-digital games may be a positive behaviour in terms of reducing cognitive decline."

Professor Ian Deary, director of the University of Edinburgh's Centre for Cognitive Ageing and Cognitive Epidemiology, said the research is "narrowing down the sorts of activities that might help to keep people sharp in older age".

"It'd be good to find out if some of these games are more potent than others," Professor Deary added. "We also point out that several other things are related to better cognitive ageing, such as being physically fit and not smoking."

Caroline Abrahams, charity director at Age UK, said that the findings of the study are "further evidence" that the decline of thinking skills in old age "doesn't have to be inevitable".

"The connection between playing board games and other non-digital games later in life and sharper thinking and memory skills adds to what we know about steps we can take to protect our cognitive health, including not drinking excess alcohol, being active and eating a healthy diet," said Ms Abrahams.

25 November 2019

The above information is reprinted with kind permission from *The Independent*.
© independent.co.uk 2020

www.independent.co.uk

How the Spanish unearthed the secret to longevity and happiness

BY Annie Bennett

Not that the Spanish need any justification for devouring Ibérico ham at every opportunity, knocking back a glass or two of wine with lunch or having dinner when many other nations are going to bed, but it must be nice to know that these and other habits are contributing to a longer and no doubt more enjoyable life.

According to the Institute for Health Metrics and Evaluation, Spaniards are set to have the best life expectancy in the world by 2040, nudging ahead of the Japanese, to reach an average of 85.8 years. In the UK, we can only expect to get to the age of 83.3, despite our obsession with counting calories, steps, and portions of fruit and vegetables.

Of course, I'm not saying Spanish people don't do that too, there is a huge diet and fitness industry, but in general they have a much more relaxed attitude when it comes to eating and drinking.

While the Mediterranean diet undoubtedly plays a big part, a key factor is likely to be the free healthcare system. Within Spain, it is the Madrileños who top the life expectancy table, probably because of the access to several of the best hospitals in the country, together with a greater percentage of high incomes.

Admittedly, the Spanish capital also has one of the worst pollution problems, which the study shows can shave years of your life. But if more people took a leaf out of the Madrileños' book and wrote off entire afternoons to sit on a sunny pavement terrace drinking wine, both health and happiness levels would soar. That's my theory anyway, and I've been merrily sticking to it for a few decades now.

After Madrid, the next two parts of Spain in the ranking are the neighbouring regions of La Rioja and Navarra, where the cuisines feature a lot more vegetables than other areas. And they produce and drink a lot of excellent wine of course. Go on a holiday where you walk or cycle from vineyard to vineyard and you could call it a health break. None of these top three is actually on the Mediterranean, by the way, but they still eat loads of fresh fish, which is zoomed from the coast in refrigerated lorries and planes, a more sophisticated version of what muleteers were doing centuries ago.

Whenever I'm asked about the differences between living in the UK and Spain, the importance of meal times is always near the top of my list. If you arrange to meet someone at two or three o'clock in Spain, you are going to have lunch, no question about it. And if you meet between nine and 11 at night, you are having dinner together, or at least going to a few tapas bars. Eating proper meals is still a big part of Spanish life and means less mindless grazing.

Big family lunches at weekends are as popular as ever, whether in the home or at a restaurant, with three, four or even five generations getting together around the table for a meal that is likely to last several hours. The benefits of this are not just about the food – which is likely to be traditional

How long will different nationalities live in 2040?

Spain: 85.8 years (1st)

Japan: 85.7 years (2nd)

Singapore: 85.4 years (3rd)

Switzerland: 85.2 years (4th)

Portugal: 84.5 years (5th)

Italy: 84.5 years (6th)

Israel: 84.4 years (7th)

France: 84.3 years (8th)

Luxembourg: 84.1 years (9th)

Australia: 84.1 years (10th)

UK: 83.3 years (23rd)

Ireland: 83.3 years (24th)

Germany: 83.2 years (25th)?

China: 81.9 years (39th)

Croatia: 80.2 years (55th)

US: 79.8 years (64th)

Mexico: 78.3 years (87th)

Egypt: 76.2 years (106th)

Russia: 75.6 years (116th)

India: 74.5 years (129th)

South Africa: 69.3 years (169th)

Lesotho: 57.3 years (195th)

– but also the mood-boosting effect of spending time with loved ones. A strong family structure means older people get more support – often living with their adult children – which means they are less likely to miss meals and health problems are spotted earlier.

But please don't feel guilty as you open your pizza box on the sofa tonight, as all the big fast food chains are present throughout Spain and show no signs of going out of business any time soon. Maybe Spaniards are living longer because they spend more time outside and sometimes take siestas on hot summer afternoons. Probably worth giving it a go if you ask me, just to be on the safe side.

13 January 2020

The above information is reprinted with kind permission from *The Telegraph*.
© Telegraph Media Group Limited 2020

www.telegraph.co.uk

Healthy habits add up to 10 disease-free years to your life, study reveals

"Healthy habits extend disease-free life by up to a decade",' reports *The Guardian*.

More people are living longer, thanks to the rise in life expectancy. The downside is that more people are living with diseases like diabetes, cancer and heart disease.

Yet many of these diseases are linked to lifestyle-related risk factors like poor diet, being overweight and smoking.

A study of more than 110,000 people assessed 5 healthy habits, and estimated how much longer people with these habits live, and also how many of those extra years are likely to be disease-free.

The study found that women who adopted 4 or 5 of the habits were likely to live an extra 10 years without cardiovascular disease (heart disease and stroke), cancer or type 2 diabetes compared with women adopting none. The corresponding figure for men was 7 years.

The markers of a healthy lifestyle used by the researchers were:

♦ not smoking

♦ having a healthy body mass index (BMI) of 18.5 to 24.9

♦ doing 30 minutes moderate to vigorous exercise a day

♦ drinking alcohol only in moderation (defined in this study as just under 2 units for women and 4 units for men daily)

♦ having a healthy diet score in the top 40% of people in the study

While the way the study was run cannot prove the healthy lifestyle directly caused the additional years of healthy life, it adds considerable weight to existing evidence that has already shown these lifestyle habits reduce the chance of disease. Find out more about leading a healthy lifestyle.

Where did the story come from?

The researchers who carried out the study were from the Harvard TH Chan School of Public Health and Harvard Medical School in the US, Erasmus Medical Centre in the Netherlands and Huazhong University of Science and Technology in China.

The study was funded by the US National Institutes of Health. It was published in the peer-reviewed British Medical Journal on an open access basis, so is free to read online.

The study was widely reported in the UK media. The reports in The Times and the Mail Online implied that having healthy habits at age 50 would lead to a longer life – but the study followed participants for many years, assessing habits every 2 years for 28 to 34 years. Long-term healthy habits, not habits at any particular age, are what counts.

What kind of research was this?

The researchers used 2 cohort studies.

Cohort studies are good ways to look at links between risk factors (such as unhealthy lifestyle habits like smoking and not exercising) and outcomes (such as getting cardiovascular disease, cancer, diabetes or dying).

(BONUS LIFE SPAN)

However, cohort studies cannot prove that the risk factors directly cause the outcomes. Other factors may be involved.

What did the research involve?

Researchers used information from 2 cohorts of men and women that were studied in the US between 1980 and 2014, the Nurses' Health Study of female nurses, and the Health Professionals Follow-up Study of male doctors, dentists and other healthcare professionals.

The women were followed up for 34 years and the men for 28 years.

During the studies, the participants completed questionnaires every 2 years that included information about their weight and height, smoking status, physical activities, alcohol intake and diet.

They were also asked whether they had been diagnosed with type 2 diabetes, cardiovascular disease or cancer (the researchers reviewed medical records to confirm diagnoses). Deaths were reported via a registry.

The researchers calculated how long people lived before being diagnosed with one of the conditions studied, according to how many healthy lifestyle factors they adopted. People were assigned a healthy lifestyle score of 0 to 5, with 5 indicating they had all 5 healthy lifestyle factors and 0 that they had none.

The researchers then used the information to construct models to estimate how long someone aged 50 could expect to live free of cardiovascular disease, diabetes or cancer, according to their healthy lifestyle score.

They also looked at which unhealthy lifestyles had most effect on the outcome, and on which diseases were most affected by lifestyle.

What were the basic results?

Overall, women and men aged 50 could expect to live another 30 to 40 years, and 75% to 84% of that time would be free of the diseases studied.

However, women and men with healthy lifestyles could expect to live longer, healthier lives. They were less likely to be diagnosed with cancer, cardiovascular disease or diabetes, and if they did get these diseases, they survived for longer after diagnosis.

The study estimates that for people aged 50:

♦ women with 4 or 5 healthy lifestyle habits can expect to live another 41.1 years, 34.4 years of which would be free of disease

♦ women with no healthy lifestyle habits can expect to live another 31.7 years, 23.7 of which would be free of disease

♦ men with 4 or 5 healthy lifestyle habits can expect to live another 39.4 years, 31.2 of which would be free of disease

♦ men with no healthy lifestyle habits can expect to live another 31.3 years, 23.5 of which would be free of disease

The people with the worst disease-free life expectancy were men who smoked heavily and men and women who were obese (body mass index over 30).

Diabetes was the condition most closely linked to lifestyle, with 90% of people diagnosed with diabetes in the study

estimated to have the condition because of unhealthy lifestyles.

Cancer was the least closely linked, with 50% of cancers estimated to be due to unhealthy lifestyles.

How did the researchers interpret the results?

The researchers said: 'We observed that a healthier lifestyle was associated with a lower risk of cancer, cardiovascular disease and diabetes, as well as mortality, with an increased total life expectancy and number of years lived free of these diseases.'

Conclusion

It is no surprise that adopting a healthy lifestyle is likely to lead to a longer life and less chance of getting diabetes, cancer or cardiovascular disease.

The study adds to the existing evidence that shows not smoking, being a healthy weight, exercising, eating well and drinking only in moderation is likely to increase our chances of living disease-free for longer.

Cohort studies cannot prove that lifestyle factors directly cause outcomes like length of life or disease, however. Other factors – such as genetics, other health conditions and socioeconomic circumstances – may also be involved. But there is already good evidence to show that the healthy lifestyle factors measured are linked to better health, even if they cannot completely eliminate disease risk.

There are other limitations to the study.

Most of the lifestyle data was self-reported, which could lead to some inaccuracy in measurement.

Diseases were self-reported, though these were medically confirmed so more likely to be reliable.

Also, the study participants were all educated healthcare professionals, so might be expected to have a healthier-than-average lifestyle. They were also mostly white and all lived in the US. We do not know if the results would apply to other groups of people.

Overall, this is good news for people who try to adopt a healthy lifestyle.

There are many reasons why some people find this harder than others. The results should encourage governments and public health authorities to try and make it easier for everyone to live healthy lives.

9 January 2020

The above information is reprinted with kind permission from the NHS.
© Crown copyright 2020

www.nhs.uk

'It's like family': the Swedish housing experiment designed to cure loneliness

A radical new scheme offers homes to different ages and backgrounds – and insists that they (safely) mingle.

By Derek Robertson

Erik Ahlsten is unequivocal. 'This is the best accommodation I've ever had.' His friend and neighbour Manfred Bacharach is equally enthusiastic. 'I really like this way of living,' he says. 'It's very much my cup of tea.'

The two are referring to their new home, Sällbo, a radical experiment in multigenerational living in Helsingborg, a small port city in southern Sweden. Its name is a portmanteau of the Swedish words for companionship (sällskap) and living (bo), and neatly encapsulates the project's goals – to combat loneliness and promote social cohesion by giving residents incentives, and the spaces, for productive interaction.

Sällbo, which opened last November, consists of 51 apartments spread over four floors of a refurbished retirement home. More than half of the 72 residents are over 70s, like Ahlsten and Bacharach; the rest are aged 18-25. All were selected after an extensive interview process to ensure a mix of personalities, backgrounds, religions, and values, and all had to sign a contract promising to spend at least two hours a week socialising with their neighbours.

'A new way to live,' proclaims Sällbo's website boldly, adding that it's where 'generations and cultures meet, with social life in the centre'. The project is administered by Helsingsborgshem, a not-for-profit housing company funded by the city council, and stems from an idea they had in 2016 amid concern about loneliness among older groups. Swedes are fiercely independent – young people start living alone earlier than anywhere in Europe – a trait that continues into old age; thanks to public policy and a wide range of municipal services many elderly people opt to remain in their own homes.

Yet a sense of isolation poses a real 'danger to health', according to the Karolinska Institute, and remains prevalent among retirees. 'Our research showed that elderly people were feeling isolated from society, and were very lonely in their everyday life,' says Dragana Curovic, the project manager at Sällbo. 'They were only mixing with others of the same age.'

At the same time, the 2015 refugee crisis meant organisations like Helsingsborgshem were under pressure to house growing numbers of people who were struggling to integrate with – and win acceptance from – Swedish society. So a plan was hatched to mix the two, with younger Swedish people acting 'as a bridge'. 'They are closer in age to the refugees, but closer in terms of culture and language to the older people,' says Curovic. 'We hoped they would bring them together.'

Although less than a year old, and despite the complications of a pandemic, the arrangement seems to be working for young and old. One resident, a 92-year-old former teacher, has been giving English lessons. Ahlsten and Bacharach have been cooking communal dinners, doing repairs and odd jobs, and driving people around; Bacharach taught one resident, an Afghan refugee, how to drive. In return, the younger residents help with modern technology and social media, and how to find information online.

'It's a real community,' says Ahlsten, 'and the mix of people works very well.' Bacharach agrees. 'It's great doing things together and enjoying other people's company,' he says. Since moving in, he's joined the gardening group, the Sunday night movie club, and learned to play Canasta. There are sign-up sheets in the communal areas and dedicated Facebook groups for all the various activities; just as importantly, there's plenty of space.

There's a gym, yoga room, a library (stocked with the residents' own books), and a large communal kitchen on every floor. The arts-and-crafts studio is stuffed with paints, wool, and other creative paraphernalia, while the residents themselves turned one space into a workshop, complete with tools and equipment (one of the pensioners, a former sea captain, has reinvented himself as a silversmith). Even the main lounge on the ground floor is a multifunctional space, with hi-fi equipment, table football, and a piano, donated by one of the residents so that 'everyone can experience its joy'; she's hoping to give lessons.

Rents vary from 4,620 to 5,850 Swedish krona (£409 to £518) per month, which is commensurate with similar-sized rent-controlled apartments in the city (private, one-bedroom rentals in the centre cost between 7,000 and 10,000 Swedish krona).

Ali Soroush, 21, an Afghan refugee, and Isabel Tomak-Eriksson, a native Swede, are one of the few couples. Soroush arrived in 2015 and is one of the refugees Helsingsborgshem had in mind when conceiving of Sällbo. He says it reminds him of his own culture, with people – particularly different generations – living and socialising together, and helping each other out. 'The whole building is like a family,' he says.

Of course, intergenerational living carries the risk of some tensions breaking out but, so far, they have been minimal.

Helsingsborgshem appointed a full-time 'host', to act as a facilitator and moderator – to 'feel the atmosphere and deflate tension' says Curovic – but they've had precious little to do. Indeed, mutual respect and understanding has flourished; there's been neither excessive partying, nor any pedantic carping.

'You can always just close your door and relax or sleep,' says Ahlsten. And while Tomak-Eriksson notes the responsibility everyone feels as a Sällbo resident, she says it's far from boring. 'Pre-corona, there were parties all the time. Every weekend it was someone's birthday or some celebration, and there were always people around – everyone had lots of visitors.'

This planned 'togetherness' has also stood the residents in good stead during the pandemic – the threat of the disease has curtailed many of Sällbo's social aspects, particularly among the elderly. There have been no cases yet, but no one is taking any chances; some are self-quarantining, and those who do continue to meet up do so in smaller groups, and in bigger areas.

'Corona has changed everything, but I've been busy,' says Ahlsten, who's been running errands and doing shopping for those reluctant to venture out into public. Likewise Soroush and Tomak-Eriksson; 'We've been offering our help to those who need it,' she says. 'All the young people have.' And while being vigilant, and following guidelines around distancing and hand hygiene, others are more sanguine. 'Not challenging, just boring,' says Bacharach on being asked how he's coped. 'We're just waiting for it to be over.'

Even before the pandemic, Sällbo had attracted attention both within Sweden and internationally. Three municipalities are working on directly implementing the concept, and many more considering similar ideas. A delegation from Canada visited in February, while others from Italy, Germany, and South Korea have been in touch regarding study missions.

With loneliness on the rise and considered a genuine health risk – Sweden's largest daily newspaper Dagens Nyheter asked earlier this year if it was 'a new epidemic' – projects such as Sällbo are seen increasingly as a holistic solution to isolation, over-reliance on public services, and the trend, even among older people, for increasingly unhealthy internet use (wifi is free in communal areas, but tenants have to pay extra to get online in their apartments).

'We hope that people see that youngsters from other countries are not to be feared, and that you can have totally normal relationships between youngsters, elderly and other people,' says Curovic of Sällbo's ultimate goal. 'We want that to spread to society in general, and increase the willingness to integrate. And it's starting to happen.'

Soroush has seen this change first hand. 'In my old apartment building, even after one and half years I didn't know any of my neighbours,' he says. 'But here, from day one, you know everyone. It feels like home.'

15 September 2020

The above information is reprinted with kind permission from *The Guardian*.
© 2020 Guardian News and Media Limited

www.theguardian.com

Seven ways to keep fit and well in older age

PA Media (Press Association)

We're all living longer than ever, so it's a good idea to think about how you can help yourself stay as fit and well as possible during those golden years. Both medics and fitness experts like Diana Moran, 'The Green Goddess' of Eighties breakfast TV, agree that much of ageing well is down to looking after yourself, keeping active – even though it's tempting not to as your joints get creakier – eating healthily and staying socially connected.

It's why every one of our Platinum Skies retirement living locations has a dedicated Lifestyle Manager on-site, who plays a vital role in offering residents everything from friendly advice, emotional support to organising regular events such as pilates.

This means our homeowners enjoy an independent lifestyle, whilst knowing that all of the help and support you may need is always on-hand. In fact, research has shown that people who live in retirement communities have healthier, more active, more social, more secure and happier lives. Whether you live independently or need a helping hand, our flexibility means we can tailor a service that perfectly suits your needs.

And if you need proof that making an effort brings results, look no further than Moran. At 81, the super-fit grandmother, who still does a daily fitness routine, has just brought out another exercise DVD, called Keep Fit And Carry On, to get older people moving – even if it's just in their chairs.

It's so important to retain as much movement as possible, however limited your physical abilities are,' says Moran. 'I know what a difference it makes. Life is so much richer if you're physically fit. Chances are you'll be mentally very fit as well.'

Tahir Masud, a professor of geriatric medicine and president of the British Geriatrics Society (bgs.org.uk), points out that keeping up good levels of physical activity can reduce the risk of dementia and depression by up to 30%, type 2 diabetes by 40%, and cut the chances of getting certain cancers, such as breast and colon cancer, by 20-30%. Being physically active also means you're 30% less likely to suffer falls. 'All the evidence shows that if you're motivated enough to do proper lifestyle measures, it can really make a difference,' he says.

Here, Moran and Masud outline seven of the best ways for older people to keep fit and healthy…

1. Keep active

One of the most important things about looking after yourself as you get older is making sure you're as active as possible, stresses Masud, who says older people should aim for 150 minutes of moderate intensity physical exercise per week, like walking, jogging or cycling, with a particular emphasis on maintaining strength and balance.

Moran's Keep Fit And Carry On DVD which she's proud to say she home-filmed herself during lockdown, is designed to get older people moving gently. 'I'm very, very aware of how exercise – moderate, I'm not talking about going to the gym and pumping iron and all that business – is important to maintain your good health,' she says.

'Joe Wicks was wonderful and motivated children in particular, but I was concerned about us older people. I realised many were all self-isolating, as I was, and many were very lonely and had a lack of a lifeline – that's why I concentrated on exercises for people with perhaps limited mobility, and those who maybe haven't exercised for a while.'

And there are numerous options for people who struggle to get out of a chair or use a wheelchair, Moran adds, including both upper and lower body exercises. 'It's surprising how much you can actually do sitting in a chair,' she says. This includes weights workouts using cans rather than dumbbells, and strengthening activities using exercise bands or even an old pair of tights.

'When you do any form of exercise, there are four immediate benefits,' Moran explains. 'The first one is strength – if you're getting up off a chair, you're using your quadriceps muscles, you're keeping your legs strong. If you're lifting a can, you're keeping your arms strong.

'The next is that physical activity and lifting things keeps you supple, and if you're getting up and moving, you're improving your stamina and your cardiovascular system. If you get it right and eat a reasonably good, mixed healthy diet, then chances are you're going to keep in shape.'

2. Minimise sedentary time

If managing proper exercise is too much, Masud says people should at least try to get up a bit more frequently if possible, rather than being too sedentary for long periods. 'You shouldn't just sit in front of the TV without getting up regularly,' he says. 'If you're watching a programme for an hour, you should get up a few times, even if it's to make a cup of tea.'

3. Avoid 'bad' things

It's an obvious one, but just because smoking and drinking haven't killed you yet doesn't mean they won't get you in the future. 'Older people need to reduce smoking and excessive alcohol,' says Masud. 'There's lots of evidence that if you want to stay healthy as you get older, you've got to cut back on those particular things.'

4. Good nutrition

Masud says the NHS Eat Well Guide (nhs.uk/live-well/eat-well/the-eatwell-guide) gives a good outline of what your diet should look like as you get older. 'The important things are to cut back on carbohydrates and sugar, but what's stressed is that an adequate amount of protein, for example eggs, meat, fish, and pulses, is really important,' he says. 'If you don't have enough protein, you've got an increased chance of becoming frail, which causes problems such as falls and other issues.'

In addition, everyone – at any age – needs to try to eat five portions of different fruit and vegetables a day, and plenty of fibre.

5. Stay connected

'Loneliness isn't a good thing for your future health,' says Masud. 'And as you get older, if you get socially isolated and lonely, it can increase the risk of heart disease, depression and dementia.'

Although the brain isn't technically a muscle, it still needs 'exercising' like one. 'If you don't use it, you'll lose it,' explains Masud. 'You start developing cognitive impairment and losing your memory.'

And lonely older people may have a higher risk of heart disease simply because having more reasons to socialise means you're more likely to get out and about, which means keeping your body and brain more active. Getting out and about also reduces the risk of obesity, which can affect the heart too.

6. Get your jabs

Older people should have the flu vaccination every year, stresses Masud, plus any other important jabs, like those for shingles and pneumonia. Talk to your doctor or pharmacist about what you might need.

7. Strengthen your bones

More than 30 years ago, Moran suffered a typical osteoporotic fracture to her wrist while ice-skating. Many years later, when she was 79, she was diagnosed with osteopenia, the condition that precedes osteoporosis. 'I know how important it is to do weight-bearing exercises,' says Moran, who also works with the Royal Osteoporosis Society (theros.org.uk) – she joined forced with the charity to write her book Beating Osteoporosis, highlighting how to reduce the risk of weaker bones.

This can include things as simple as 'walking, gardening, putting weight on your spine, hips and legs and lifting up, lifting your grandchildren', she adds. 'You're putting weight on your wrists, and your wrists, hip and spine are the areas where you could be affected by osteoporosis and have a fracture.'

26 August 2020

The above information is reprinted with kind permission from Platinum Skies.
© 2020 Platinum Skies

www.platinumskies.co.uk

Key Facts

- In 2018, there were 11.9 million residents in Great Britain aged 65 years and over, representing 18% of the total population. (page 1)

- The current record holder (of the longest ever recorded lifespan) is the French woman Jeanne Calment, who died on August 4, 1997, aged 122 years, five months. (page 4)

- Even though the average global life expectancy is still below 80 years, almost two-thirds of today's newborns will live to see the next century. (page 5)

- The top three countries in terms of life expectancy are all in Asia—Singapore, Japan, South Korea—followed by European countries and Chile. (page 5)

- Life expectancy in the UK is currently 79.6 years for men and 83.2 years for women. (page 8)

- Japanese women have a life expectancy of 87.3 years – the second highest in the world after Hong Kong – while male life expectancy in Japan is the third highest internationally, well ahead of the US and UK. (page 10)

- Obesity rates in Japan are very low, with fewer than 5% classed as obese compared to nearly 28% of people in the UK and 36% in the USA. (page 10)

- Since 1961 Japan has had universal healthcare, with equal and universal access to healthcare for all through a health insurance scheme which is paid for by government, employers and individuals. (page 11)

- In South Africa the average retirement age is 60. This is currently the lowest in the world. (page 12)

- The retirement age in the UK is currently 65. (page 13)

- In South Korea, both men and women work on average 13 years longer than the official retirement age of 60. So with an average retirement age of 73, South Koreans currently have the longest working lives in the world. (page 14)

- Research from over 50s finance provider SunLife suggests that more than seven million over-50s have no private pension and more than eight million don't think they have enough money to fund their retirement. (page 18)

- In Europe, 44% of older workers, and 64% in the UK said they were concerned about age discrimination (page 19)

- Women experience ageism from around the age of 40 in the UK, compared with men who experience it from 45. (page 19)

- A study by PwC estimates that OECD (Organization for Economic Cooperation and Development) members could increase their total GDP by around $3.5 trillion by following New Zealand's example of having one of the highest employment rates in the world for older workers (55 and over). (page 19)

- From the third decade of life we begin to lose muscle mass. Losses of between 30 to 50% have been reported between the ages of 40 and 80. (page 20)

- The Royal Voluntary Service charity found that 11% (or 955,464) people aged 70 and over in the UK confess to relying on ready meals and convenience foods to keep them fed with nearly a quarter (23%) saying they skip their daily meals at least three times a week. (page 25)

- Over one in five over 70s (22%) stated they ate all their daily meals alone each week, rising to over a quarter (26%) of people over 80. Of those who eat most of their meals alone, 38% admit they miss having company at meal times. (page 25)

- In the UK alone, 15,000 people are over 100 years of age. (page 26)

- Local authorities spent more than £22bn on social care in 2018-19, which is less than the amount spent a decade ago, according to health policy think tank The King's Fund. (page 30)

- The Local Government Association estimates that the UK faces a social care funding gap of almost £4bn by 2024. (page 30)

- Most Britons don't believe they will require support as they age, despite extensive evidence to the contrary. Around 70 per cent of older people in England, for example, receive some sort of care, with many more needing it but not receiving support. (page 30)

- In England, 167,000 older people and their families are estimated to fund their own care because they do not qualify for free or subsidised support. (page 31)

- According to the Institute for Health Metrics and Evaluation, Spaniards are set to have the best life expectancy in the world by 2040, nudging ahead of the Japanese, to reach an average of 85.8 years. (page 34)

- Keeping up good levels of physical activity can reduce the risk of dementia and depression by up to 30%, type 2 diabetes by 40%, and cut the chances of getting certain cancers, such as breast and colon cancer, by 20-30%. Being physically active also means you're 30% less likely to suffer falls. (page 38)

Ageing

As you get older your body experiences some changes. This can include the skin wrinkling and getting thinner, less body fat being stored and your bones and muscles becoming weaker. Your memory may also get worse as you age, and your immune system will not be able to fight disease as easily. This is because the cells in your body gradually become damaged and are no longer able to replace themselves. Although ageing can`t be avoided entirely, you can put off the effects of ageing by living a healthy lifestyle.

Ageing population

A population whose average age is rising. This can be caused by increased life expectancy, for example following significant medical advances, or by falling birth rates, for example due to the introduction of contraception. However, the higher the proportion of older people within a population, the lower the birth rate will become due to there being fewer people of childbearing age.

Ageism

The poor or unfair treatment of someone because of their age. Ageism can affect a person`s confidence, job prospects, financial situation and quality of life.

Centenarian

A person who has reached the age of 100. In the UK, the Queen sends out a special message to British citizens who celebrate their 100th birthday.

Dementia

Dementia is one of the main causes of disability in later life and mainly affects people over the age of 65. It can, however, affect younger people too; there are about 800,000 people in the UK with dementia, and of these over 17,000 people are under the age of 65. Symptoms of dementia include memory loss (particularly short-term; long-term memory generally remains quite good), mood changes (e.g. being more withdrawn) and communication problems.

Demographic changes (ageing population/grey population)

Demographics refer to the structure of a population. We are currently experiencing an increase in our ageing population. People are living longer thanks to advancements in medical treatment and care. Soon, the world will have more older people than children. This means that the need for long-term care is rising.

Discrimination

Unfair treatment of someone because of the group/class they belong to.

Elder abuse

Physical, emotional or sexual harm inflicted upon an elderly adult. Elder abuse also includes their financial exploitation or neglect of their welfare by people who are directly responsible for their care.

Loneliness

A feeling of being alone and isolated. Often those without social contact will feel lonely, but it is possible to feel lonely even when surrounded by others.

Pension

When someone reaches retirement age, they are entitled to receive a regular pension payment from the government. This payment takes the place of a salary. Many people choose to pay into a private pension fund throughout their career, in order to save extra money for when they retire. Often, employers also pay into a pension fund for their employees. The State Pension Age is gradually increasing. The Pensions Act 2011 will see the State Pension Age for both men and women increase to 66 by October 2020 to `keep pace with increases in longevity (people living longer)`.

Poverty

Peter Townsend offers this definition of poverty: 'Individuals, families and groups in the population can be said to be in poverty when they lack the resources to obtain the types of diet, participate in the activities, and have the living conditions and amenities which are customary, or are at least widely encouraged and approved, in the societies in which they belong.'

Retirement

The time in a person's life when they stop work completely.

Social care

Refers to non-medical care for the disabled, ill and elderly who find it difficult to look after themselves. Social care provides care, support and assistance to allow people to live their lives as fully as possible by helping them with everyday tasks they can`t do on their own. This allows people to take part in an active lifestyle as some people may need help to live in their home, get washed and dressed or go out and about to meet friends.

Social isolation

Social isolation describes the absence of social contact and can lead to loneliness.

Widow/Widower

A widow is a woman whose husband has died. A man whose wife has died is called a widower.

Activities

Brainstorming

♦ What is meant by the term 'ageing population'?

♦ Why is our population ageing?

♦ In the UK , what is the average life expectancy for:

· a man

· a woman?

♦ In the UK, what is the default retirement age (the age at which you qualify for a state pension)?

♦ Are populations ageing all over the world?

♦ What do you think are the major factors contributing to increased life expectancy over the last 100 years?

Research

♦ Do some research to find out about the quality of life for the elderly population of another country. How are they treated within their communities and cared for by their governments? When you have chosen your country and completed your research, create a PowerPoint presentation and share your findings with the rest of your class.

♦ Look online for studies or news articles reporting about ageism in the UK. How many stories or examples did you find? Share and compare with the rest of your class.

♦ Do some research about care homes. You could look at care home websites, or maybe arrange a visit to a care home local to you. Perhaps you already know someone in a care home and could ask them about their experiences?

♦ Read the article on page 26: *Robots to be used in UK care homes to help reduce loneliness*. In small groups, discuss the pros and cons of this proposed solution to loneliness. Do you think it will work? Think about other methods that could be used to tackle this problem. When you have an idea, present it to the rest of the class.

♦ Conduct a search online and find the oldest living man and oldest living woman in the world today.

Design

♦ Choose one of the articles from this book and create an illustration to accompany it.

♦ Create a poster highlighting the key issues from the article on page 25.

♦ Read the article on page 20: *How biscuits enriched with protein could keep the UK's ageing population strong*. Imagine you work for a company that has just created such a biscuit. Create an advertising campaign aimed at older people promoting this product. Give your biscuit a brand name and a slogan and design a billboard for it.

♦ Design a 'retirement home of the future'. Think about the facilities you might need as you age, but make it fun as well as practical. Include a brief explanation of the features you have included.

♦ Draw and describe a stereotypical old person. Compare your drawing with others and explain why you drew what you did. Now draw and describe how you think people from an older generation see you. Look carefully at each drawing and discuss the idea of perceptions and stereotypes and how these change with age. Is it harmful to discriminate against others because of their age?

Oral

♦ Choose one of the illustrations from this book and, in pairs, discuss what you think the artist is trying to portray.

♦ In small groups, discuss what you might do to help an elderly neighbour who is extremely lonely.

♦ Plan a lesson in which you will teach an older person who has never used a computer about the basics of the internet. Remember that basic skills that come naturally to you may be completely alien to them, so think carefully about the steps you will need to cover. Also consider what this person might find most useful about having a computer and access to the internet.

Reading/writing

♦ Write a definition of the term 'age discrimination'.

♦ Imagine you are someone of retirement age writing a letter to a younger person explaining to them how important it is to plan for your retirement. Advise your young friend to think about finances and pensions.

♦ Read the articles on pages 27 and 37. Both describe social experiments where older and younger generations live together. What were the benefits and drawbacks of such a living arrangement? Overall, was it a positive experience for everyone? Write 500 words about your thoughts on this.

♦ In pairs, write a list of five positive things you can learn from older people, and a list of five positive things older people can learn from you. Share your ideas with the rest of the class.

Index

Acknowledgements

The publisher is grateful for permission to reproduce the material in this book. While every care has been taken to trace and acknowledge copyright, the publisher tenders its apology for any accidental infringement or where copyright has proved untraceable. The publisher would be pleased to come to a suitable arrangement in any such case with the rightful owner.

The material reproduced in *ISSUES* books is provided as an educational resource only. The views, opinions and information contained within reprinted material in *ISSUES* books do not necessarily represent those of Independence Educational Publishers and its employees.

Images

Cover image courtesy of iStock. All other images courtesy of Pixabay and Unsplash, except pages 6:Freepik, 8: karlyukar from Freepik, 27: Rawpixel from Freepik

Illustrations

Simon Kneebone: pages 3, 12 & 29. Angelo Madrid: pages 9, 18 & 35.

Additional acknowledgements

With thanks to the Independence team: Shelley Baldry, Danielle Lobban, Jackie Staines and Jan Sunderland.

Tracy Biram

Cambridge, September 2020